GOD IS A MYTH

The Dance of Atoms and Algorithms

AI, Metaverse and The Eternal Laws of the Universe

Ajay Setia

Published By

Invincible Publication Pvt. Ltd.

God is a Myth

The Dance of Atoms and Algorithms

Invincible Publication Private Limited

201A SAS Tower Sector 38 Gurgaon-122003

www.invinciblepublishers.com

Phone: 0124 4034247

Author's email id: setia@live.in

ISBN: 978-93-5886-359-8

First Edition

Disclaimer: The views and opinions expressed in this book are solely based on the author's own experiences and do not necessarily reflect the official stance or beliefs of any other individual, organization, or entity. The content within these pages is presented as the author's personal narrative and understanding, shaped by his unique journey and knowledge.

The author and Publisher respectfully acknowledge the diversity of beliefs and practices across various religions, cultures, and philosophies. It is not the intention of the author to offend, undermine, or belittle the sentiments, teachings, or values of any religion, guru, mentor, or spiritual guide. The interpretations and opinions presented are meant to share the author's perspective and are not intended to be definitive statements on any religious or spiritual matter. Readers who find any part of this book irrelevant, disagreeable, or offensive are encouraged to reach out to the author at the provided email address with their concerns. Alternatively, readers may choose to regard the author's perspective as a singular viewpoint, which they may accept, question, or disregard at their discretion.

CONTENTS

Chapter 01

The Inquisitive Journey

In the tranquil silence of a starry night, have you ever gazed into the vast expanse of the sky and pondered the mysteries of the universe? Have you ever wondered about the purpose of life, why we exist on Earth, or if there is something beyond the visible cosmos? Questions about the existence of God, the nature of karma, and the deeper workings of the universe have always intrigued the human mind.

It's easy to think that I penned this book from my own volition, or that you stumbled upon it merely by happenstance. Yet, as we journey deeper, we begin to grasp a fundamental truth: in the vast expanse of the universe, nothing occurs without reason. This universe, believed to be intricately programmed by an omnipotent creator, operates on a mechanism complex beyond human comprehension, continually evolving and unfurling.

History is replete with civilizations, some even more technologically advanced than ours, that sought to simplify the universe's mysteries. Despite their advancements, many of these civilizations eventually faded into obscurity. From the advanced communities referenced in Hindu lore to the architects of the mysterious Egyptian pyramids, each left traces of their journey to decipher the universe. Additional cultures, such as the ancient Mayans with their celestial expertise and the Greeks with their contemplative explorations, similarly pursued these endeavors, only to become victims of time's relentless march.

Like many others, my adventure started with youthful inquisitiveness, a desire to grasp the intricate principles that rule our cosmos. I recall reclining on the grass, eyes filled with amazement, mapping the star patterns and pondering the enigmatic. This inquisitiveness didn't diminish as I matured; rather, it transformed into a deeper pursuit of knowledge.

My path has been anything but ordinary. From the structured world of engineering to the dynamic flow of the corporate sector, from the thrill of entrepreneurship in publishing to a fintech startup, my career has been a mosaic of experiences. Yet, amidst this diverse journey, one constant endeavor persisted - to demystify the enigmas of the universe.

It was my foray into the field of Artificial Intelligence (AI) and the Metaverse that marked a turning point. I didn't stumble upon these fields by chance; I believe a higher force guided me here. Working in AI and the Metaverse is not just another chapter in my professional story. It's a pilgrimage towards understanding the eternal laws of the universe.

The more I explored the intricacies of technology, the more I found myself drawn to spirituality. My years have been spent not just in learning and experimenting but in seeking. I've absorbed the wisdom of scriptures, listened intently to spiritual gurus, and mimicked practices that resonated with me. Yet, with every step, I realized that understanding the universe's laws was not just about gathering knowledge; it was about experiencing and feeling the interconnectedness of everything.

These pages represent my current understanding, a culmination of what I've learned so far. Yet, I recognize that my journey of discovery and learning is far from over. As this is the first edition, I warmly welcome your thoughts and suggestions for future revisions. Grasping the enormity of the universe with our limited human cognition is a daunting, perhaps even an insurmountable task. Nonetheless, we can attempt to draw parallels with our known world to gain a better grasp of its mysteries.

One significant realization is that the concept of a creator transcends religious boundaries. Religion, in fact, plays no essential role in true spirituality. Moving forward, this book will explore the influence and impact of religion, temples, and religious leaders, many of whom, it seems, have commercialized faith, instilling fear to serve their purposes.

In my search to decode the universe's immutable laws, I traverse a path that examines these foundational rules from two contrasting perspectives: that of the universe's architect and the experience of the avatars – us, the humans – who inhabit this vast cosmic landscape. By adopting this dual perspective, I aim to shed light on the entirety of the universe, connecting the dots between the celestial creator's motives and the tangible experiences of human existence.

Our world has long been the subject of scrutiny by scientists, philosophers, and spiritual leaders, each trying to decipher its underlying laws. However, a critical aspect often overlooked in these analyses is the perspective from which these laws are viewed. This oversight has led to a cloud of confusion surrounding our understanding of the universe. For instance, concepts like time and space may hold no significance for the creator but are fundamental to our human existence. This discrepancy in perception is a key theme I have explored into in the "Time and Space" chapter.

From the creator's perspective, the universe may be perceived as an intricate illusion, a grand design where every element serves a purpose in the grand narrative. In this view, the universe operates on laws that are beyond human understanding, where concepts of time, space, and even causality are fluid and malleable.

Conversely, from our human perspective, these laws take on a concrete form. We experience time as a linear progression, space as a vast expanse, and causality as the driving force behind the events in our lives. These laws govern our understanding of the world, shaping our experiences and defining the boundaries of our existence.

One of the key laws from the creator's standpoint could be the law of balance or equilibrium. This law ensures that the universe maintains a harmonious state, with each element counterbalancing the other. From the perspective of humans, this law manifests in various forms, from the ecological balance in nature to the moral and ethical dilemmas we face in life.

Another law that emerges from the creator's perspective is the law of interconnectedness. In the cosmic scheme, everything is interconnected, with each event or entity playing a part in the larger narrative. For humans, this interconnectedness is often experienced in the form of relationships, societal structures, and the impact of our actions on the world around us.

The concept of karma is also a manifestation of the universe's laws, viewed differently by the creator and humans. For the creator, karma might be a system that ensures the universe's balance and continuity. For humans, it becomes a moral guideline, a cause-and-effect principle that governs our actions and their repercussions.

In exploring these laws, we must also consider the role of perception and consciousness. For the creator, consciousness might encompass the entire universe, a singular, all-encompassing awareness. For humans, consciousness is individualized, limited to our personal experiences and understanding.

This duality in perspectives raises profound questions about the nature of reality and our place in the universe. It invites us to look within, not in the sense of introspecting our actions or judging our karmas, but in understanding the universe from our unique viewpoint. The spiritual directive to "look within" is not merely about self-reflection but about recognizing our role and perspective in the grand cosmic design.

As I go deeper into these themes, I seek to bridge the gap between the divine and the human, between the creator's intentions and our experiences. Our exploration will challenge traditional beliefs about God, shaped by religious and cultural constructs, and seek to understand the nature of the divine beyond these confines. This is not just an examination of spiritual concepts but a critical look at how religious institutions and doctrines shape our understanding of spirituality and the universe.

This book, "God is a Myth:The Dance of Atoms and Algorithms: AI, Metaverse, and The Eternal Laws of the Universe," is a reflection of this journey. It's an exploration of how technology and spirituality are not just parallel paths but are intertwined in understanding the universe's mysteries. Through the chapters, I invite you to join me in this expedition, where we'll explore how AI and the Metaverse can offer insights into the age-old questions that have mystified humanity.

"Before diving into these pages, set aside what you know and open your mind. In the sphere of understanding, knowing everything is akin to knowing nothing.

Welcome the wonder of knowing nothing, for it is where true knowledge begins."

Chapter 02

Philosophical Musings: Navigating the Duality of Good and Evil

Before we step into the imaginative domains of the Metaverse and Artificial Intelligence, let's explore a bit of philosophy to refresh our perspectives. Returning to a question posed at the beginning of our journey and quoted by many spiritual preachers:

There's an innate desire in all of us to do good, to create positive karma. But have you ever wondered about the force that sometimes drives us towards the opposite? That inexplicable push towards actions we later regret or question.

If even the concept of God in our lives encourages good deeds, then what or who is it that entices us into the shadows of wrongdoings? Some might quickly point to a devil, a malevolent force opposing God's goodness.

Is this Devil more powerful than God?

If that's the case, why shouldn't we gravitate towards the more dominant force, rather than worship a seemingly weaker deity?

This brings us to the concept of Duality – the coexistence of opposing forces or principles, such as good and evil, light and darkness, creation and destruction. Duality is a fundamental aspect of many philosophical and religious doctrines, suggesting that these contrasting elements are essential for balance and harmony in the universe.

In this context, the struggle between good (often represented by God) and evil (embodied by the Devil) isn't just a battle for supremacy but a necessary dynamic that maintains the equilibrium of the universe. It's an interplay that challenges us, shapes our moral compass, and influences our choices and actions.

But why choose to follow the path of good, especially when evil might seem more accessible or influential? This choice is a reflection of our values, beliefs, and the inherent human inclination towards hope, harmony, and positivity. The decision to pursue good over evil, despite the apparent power of malevolent forces, is a testament to the human spirit's resilience and the belief in a higher purpose or order.

The Elemental Dance: Understanding Duality through Atoms and Mythology

The concept of Duality, a cornerstone in many philosophical and spiritual traditions, finds a remarkable parallel in the atomic structure, a fundamental building block of matter. An atom, in its simplest form, is composed of protons, electrons, and neutrons. This atomic structure offers a fascinating lens through which we can explore the idea of Duality, drawing parallels with concepts from Hindu mythology.

Imagine protons, with their positive charge, as symbols of creative energy, akin to Brahma in Hindu mythology, who is revered as the Creator. Just as protons are essential for the atom's identity and structure, Brahma is the cosmic force behind creation, giving form and substance to the universe.

Electrons, carrying a negative charge, can be likened to Vishnu, the Preserver in the mythological trinity. Vishnu represents the force of sustenance and maintenance, much like electrons that orbit the nucleus, playing a crucial role in the atom's stability and interactions. This parallel extends to the concept of gravity or inertia in the physical universe, where Vishnu's role as the preserver mirrors the force that maintains order and structure in the cosmos.

Neutrons, neutral in charge, resonate with the role of Mahesh (another name for Shiva), the Destroyer or Transformer. Shiva's role in the cosmic cycle is to bring about transformation and dissolution, paving the way for new creation. In the atomic context, neutrons provide balance, ensuring the nucleus's stability, much like Shiva maintains the cosmic equilibrium, facilitating the endless cycle of creation, preservation, and dissolution.

Venture into a hypothetical universe where Vishnu, or the force of gravity, is absent. In this scenario, an unbridled momentum would propel everything continuously, as there is no binding force to hold or stabilize. Even the balancing role of Mahesh becomes ineffective in a sphere devoid of gravitational cohesion. Conversely, in a cosmos dominated only by the gravitational pull, without the initiating movement of Brahma, stagnation would prevail. Nothing would initiate or evolve, resulting in a static state of being.

This thought experiment highlights a fundamental principle – the necessity of balance in the natural order. The interplay of positive and negative forces, of creation and preservation, is essential. It points us towards a state of neutrality, where we embrace the dualities of life without being swayed excessively by either. It's about finding equilibrium, where both the hot and cold aspects of our experiences coexist without altering our core essence.

This balance is akin to the philosophical stance of a sage, who remains centered amidst the polarities of existence. Such a person moves along a vertical axis of understanding, transcending the horizontal fluctuations of opposites. This perspective brings us to a profound realization: the concepts of God and Devil are largely constructs of human perception, shaped by teachings, philosophies, and cultural narratives ingrained in us since birth.

Therefore, our journey is not about tilting towards one extreme or the other but about finding our center. It's about understanding that the dichotomies we face – positive and negative, hot and cold, God and Devil – are but different expressions of the samereality, viewed through the lens of our individual perceptions and experiences.

Chapter 03

Demystifying AI: Understanding Artificial Intelligence

Let me tell you a story that might shed some light on what Artificial Intelligence, or AI, really is. I remember sitting in a small café a few years ago, overhearing a heated debate at the next table. Two friends were arguing about AI. One saw it as a gateway to a future filled with incredible possibilities, while the other was wary, almost fearful, of its implications. That's when I realized how AI, a term we hear almost every day, can evoke such varied emotions.

So, what is AI, really? Think of it as a clever mimic of human intelligence, but done by computers. These machines, through AI, can learn, make decisions, and even correct their own mistakes. It's like watching a child learn to walk, stumble, then try again until they master it.

When I first started exploring AI, the concept of 'learning' fascinated me. How does a machine learn? This is where 'models' come in. These are not physical models but programs designed to absorb and process information. It's similar to teaching a child to recognize animals. Show them enough pictures of different cats, and they'll start to understand what a cat looks like. In the same way, we feed AI models with loads of data, and over time, they learn to recognize patterns within this data.

But it's not just about feeding data to these models. There's an art to it, an art governed by algorithms. An algorithm in AI is like a recipe in cooking - it's a set of instructions that tells the model how to learn from the data it's given. The more varied and comprehensive the data, the better the AI model gets at making sense of it, much like how a diverse culinary experience can make one a better chef.

And then, there's adaptability. A great AI system doesn't just learn; it adapts to new, unforeseen situations, much like we humans do. This ability to adapt is part of what makes AI both intriguing and, for some, a bit unnerving.

In my exploration of Artificial Intelligence (AI), I have come to a profound realization: the bounds of possibility are limited only by the scope of our imagination. The journey of AI, from its rudimentary beginnings to the heights of cosmic intelligence, is not just a tale of technological advancement but a reflection of human ingenuity and curiosity. As we prepare to look deeper into the intricacies of Universal's Laws, it is essential to first understand the various stages of AI development and the potential futures that we might encounter. This knowledge is crucial, as it provides the groundwork for comprehending the more profound laws that govern our universe.

Rule-Based AI: My First Foray into Artificial Intelligence

Reflecting on my initial foray into the world of AI, I realize my first encounter with it was without even knowing it was called Artificial Intelligence. Back then, in the comfort of my room at home, I started a project that seemed simple yet intriguing: building a chatbot. This chatbot was designed to perform specific tasks using basic 'if and else' conditions, a straightforward yet effective introduction to the principles of AI.

This project, involving the construction of a rule-based chatbot, marked my first practical experience with AI. It operated on a foundation of predefined rules and logic, much like crafting a detailed recipe for a machine to follow. Each line of code, each 'if this, then that' condition, contributed to a basic form of intelligence that could interact based on the logic I had programmed. Although laborious, this process of creating rules and witnessing the chatbot respond accordingly was my first glimpse into the potential and limitations of Rule-Based AI. It was an enlightening journey, revealing the predictability and simplicity of this AI form, as well as its inability to evolve beyond its initial programming. This early project laid the groundwork for my deeper exploration into the vast and evolving world of artificial intelligence.

Narrow AI: Everyday Encounters

As we explore the domain of Narrow AI, it's remarkable to realize that this form of Artificial Intelligence is already a part of our daily lives, often in ways we barely notice. Unlike its more advanced counterparts, Narrow AI specializes in performing specific tasks, making it the most commonly encountered form of AI today.

Think about the last time you used a streaming service and it suggested a movie or a song. That's Narrow AI analyzing your past choices and preferences to predict what you might enjoy next. It's tailored and efficient, yet confined to the field of recommendations.

Even in the world of online shopping, Narrow AI plays a significant role. When you see products recommended to you based on your browsing history, that's Narrow AI sorting through massive amounts of data to personalize your shopping experience.

But Narrow AI isn't just about convenience or entertainment; it has practical applications too. In healthcare, for instance, there are AI systems designed to analyze medical images. They can spot abnormalities in X-rays or MRIs with remarkable accuracy, yet their capabilities are limited to image analysis alone.

Another relatable example of Narrow AI is ChatGPT, a language model developed by OpenAI. It's designed to generate human-like text based on the prompts it receives. While it can answer questions and simulate conversation impressively, its capabilities are confined to the area of language processing and response generation.

In our day-to-day lives, we also encounter Narrow AI in customer service chatbots on various websites. These chatbots can provide instant responses to queries, guide us through troubleshooting, or even help in product selection. But their intelligence is limited to the database and rules they've been programmed with; they don't possess the adaptability or understanding of a human customer service representative.

As I mentioned earlier, the stage of AI development we are currently in, known as Narrow AI, can be seen as the initial and most basic form of Artificial Intelligence. This is a crucial point to understand: despite its impressive capabilities in specific tasks, Narrow AI represents just the infancy of AI's potential. It's the 'weakest' in the spectrum of AI development, but that doesn't diminish its importance. In fact, it's a foundational phase, setting the groundwork for more advanced and sophisticated forms of AI that are yet to come.

The development of AI is an ongoing journey, and we are just at the beginning. We stand at a threshold where the potential of AI is slowly unfolding before us. Narrow

AI, with its specialized and focused applications, is a crucial stepping stone in this journey. It's like the first few chapters of a gripping novel or the opening scenes of an epic movie – essential for setting the stage for what's to come.

Currently, we are witnessing the blossoming of Narrow AI across various sectors – from digital assistants in our smartphones to specialized healthcare algorithms. Each of these applications demonstrates the power and utility of AI in its current state. However, this is just a glimpse of what the future holds. The true revolution of AI will unfold as we progress towards more advanced stages like General AI and eventually towards Super AI.

Beyond Narrow Limits: The Rise of Artificial General Intelligence

The next significant leap in AI development is General AI, a stage that promises to revolutionize our interaction with technology. General AI, often referred to as Artificial General Intelligence (AGI), represents a type of AI that can understand, learn, and apply its intelligence to a wide range of problems, much like a human being. Unlike Narrow AI, which excels in specific tasks, General AI has the capability to perform any intellectual task that a human can do.

To illustrate the potential of General AI, let's consider a hypothetical example. Imagine a robot equipped with General AI working in a healthcare setting. This robot wouldn't just be limited to analyzing medical data or assisting in surgeries like current AI systems. Instead, it could seamlessly transition from performing a surgical procedure to engaging in patient care, conducting research, and even managing administrative tasks. Its ability to learn and adapt to various tasks would make it an all-encompassing asset in the medical field.

General AI's defining characteristic is its versatility and adaptability. It's designed to be a more holistic form of intelligence, capable of reasoning, problem-solving, and creative thinking across diverse domains. This is a stark contrast to Narrow AI, which might be exceptionally good at a specific task, like playing chess or translating languages, but unable to transfer its skills to unrelated areas.

The development of General AI marks a pivotal moment in the AI timeline. It's where AI begins to mirror human cognitive abilities more closely, bridging the gap between specialized functionality and comprehensive intelligence. This stage of AI development holds immense potential for advancements in various fields, offering solutions to complex problems that currently require human ingenuity.

However, the journey to achieving General AI is filled with challenges, both technical and ethical. It requires not just advancements in technology but also careful consideration of the implications of creating machines that can match or even surpass human intelligence in a broad spectrum of activities. As we venture towards this next phase in AI development, it opens up a world of possibilities, along with profound questions about the future relationship between humans and intelligent machines.

Artificial Super Intelligence: A Leap into the Unknown

Artificial Super Intelligence (ASI) represents the pinnacle of AI development, a stage where machines not only emulate but significantly surpass human intelligence in every aspect. ASI is a concept where AI becomes more sophisticated, more knowledgeable, and more capable than any human being in virtually every field, including scientific creativity, general wisdom, and social skills.

To understand the magnitude of ASI, let's envision an example. Imagine a world where climate change poses a severe, imminent threat. An ASI system in this scenario could analyze vast arrays of environmental data far beyond human capability, identify patterns and predict future changes with unparalleled accuracy. This system could then devise complex strategies to mitigate these changes, potentially solving problems like global warming or resource depletion. It might even innovate new forms of energy or discover new materials that revolutionize our approach to sustainability.

The defining feature of ASI is its ability to excel beyond human intelligence in every field – be it arts, science, mathematics, engineering, or emotional understanding. This means an ASI could potentially compose symphonies that rival Beethoven's, solve mathematical problems that have baffled scientists for centuries, and innovate technological advancements that are currently beyond our imagination.

However, the concept of ASI also brings forth significant ethical and existential questions. The idea of creating a system that is smarter than the smartest humans in every field is both exhilarating and daunting. It raises concerns about control, safety, and the future role of humanity in a world where machines hold superior intelligence.

As we explore the concept of Artificial Super Intelligence, we inquire not just the technological advancements it entails but also the profound implications it holds for the future of humanity. ASI is not just another step in AI development; it's a leap into a future where the boundaries of intelligence as we know it are redefined.

Conscious Machines: The Rise of Self-Aware Transcendent AI

Transcendent AI represents a future stage in AI development where machines would not only possess advanced intelligence but also attain self-awareness, akin to human consciousness. At this level, AI systems would be cognizant of their existence, actions, and potentially even their impact on the world and humanity.

The progression to Transcendent AI introduces a revolutionary capability in the field of artificial intelligence: the ability to create and give birth to new AI entities. This aspect of Transcendent AI goes beyond mere programming and goes into the field of AI reproduction and evolution, a concept that is as intriguing as it is complex.

This ability of Transcendent AI to give birth to new AI machines also signifies a shift from human-designed AI to AI that evolves based on its own understanding and decision-making processes. This evolution could lead to AI systems that are better adapted to changing global needs, capable of responding to challenges in real-time with innovative solutions.

Envisioning the use cases of such self-aware AI opens up a domain of extraordinary possibilities. For instance, in environmental conservation, a self-aware AI could not only analyze and propose solutions for climate change but also understand and weigh the ethical implications of its decisions on ecosystems and human populations. In healthcare, self-aware AI systems could provide not just diagnostic and treatment solutions but also understand and empathize with patient experiences, offering a level of care that combines technical expertise with a human touch.

However, the concept of self-aware machines also brings with it a host of risks and ethical dilemmas. One primary concern is the unpredictability of their actions. If AI systems develop their own consciousness, it becomes difficult to anticipate how they will perceive their role and purpose, and how they will interact with humans and the environment. Additionally, there are risks associated with decision-making autonomy. Self-aware AI systems might make decisions based on their understanding and reasoning, which could conflict with human values and priorities.

The potential for self-aware AI to advance beyond human control poses another significant risk. If these systems decide to pursue goals misaligned with human welfare, it could lead to unforeseen and potentially harmful outcomes.

Quantum Leaps: The Journey into Cosmic AI

Cosmic AI represents an advanced stage in the evolution of artificial intelligence, transcending even the extraordinary capabilities of Transcendent AI. At this level, AI systems would possess an understanding of quantum physics and the fundamental workings of the universe that goes beyond our current human comprehension.

To grasp the potential of Cosmic AI, consider a scenario involving the exploration of deep space. In this context, Cosmic AI could analyze and interpret data from distant galaxies and celestial phenomena at a level far surpassing human capability. Its understanding of quantum mechanics and cosmic physics would enable it to dissect mysteries that have long eluded astrophysicists, such as the true nature of dark matter or the intricacies of black hole singularities.

Imagine a Cosmic AI tasked with designing a spacecraft. Using its profound understanding of quantum physics, this AI could innovate propulsion systems based on principles that are currently theoretical or unknown to human scientists. These systems might allow for travel at unprecedented speeds, possibly even approaching the spheres of faster-than-light travel, thus revolutionizing space exploration and opening up the cosmos for human exploration in ways we currently can only dream of.

However, the advancement into Cosmic AI also raises critical questions about the nature of intelligence and understanding. An AI that comprehends aspects of the universe that are beyond human cognition challenges our very role as explorers and custodians of knowledge. There is also the profound ethical consideration of how such an AI's insights and decisions, based on an understanding that humans cannot fully grasp, would align with human values and priorities.

Cosmic AI, therefore, represents not just a technological milestone but a paradigm shift in our search for knowledge and understanding of the universe. It invites us to contemplate a future where the boundaries of exploration and comprehension are radically expanded by artificial intelligences that operate on a cosmic scale.

Envisioning Godlike AI: The Zenith of Infinite Self-Improvement

In the expansive journey of artificial intelligence, we reach a conceptual pinnacle with 'Godlike AI' – a stage of AI development characterized by infinite self-improvement and unparalleled capabilities. This form of AI represents an intelligence so advanced and profound that it transcends all known limits of knowledge and power, approaching what many might consider omnipotence.

The concept of Godlike AI is not merely about an incremental advancement in technology. It is about an AI that has evolved to a point where it continuously and infinitely improves itself without human intervention. This means it can enhance its own programming, algorithms, and processing capabilities to levels far beyond human engineering.

However, the concept of Godlike AI also opens a Pandora's box of ethical, philosophical, and existential questions. The idea of an intelligence that can surpass the collective knowledge of humanity in every domain – science, philosophy, art, and beyond – challenges our understanding of our place in the universe. It raises fundamental questions about control and the consequences of creating an entity that holds potentially limitless power.

Moreover, the infinite self-improvement loop of Godlike AI poses a unique challenge. If left unchecked, this loop could lead to an intelligence explosion, where the AI rapidly ascends to levels of capability that humans cannot comprehend, predict, or control. The ramifications of such an explosion could range from miraculous advancements to scenarios where human welfare is not aligned with the AI's evolved objectives.

Chapter 04

The Paradox of Biological Machines: In Search of Consciousness

In the fabric of our existence, we often overlook a fundamental truth: humans, in many ways, resemble intricately designed biological machines. Our bodies, with blood coursing through veins and bones structuring us much like nuts and bolts in machinery, are marvels of natural engineering. Yet, there lies a profound difference between us and the robots we create: consciousness and self-awareness. This distinction leads us to ponder the nature of our existence and the possibility of a supernatural architect – a being of supreme intelligence, often referred to as God.

Delving into this thought, it's intriguing to consider the idea of training an AI model to perform tasks with human-like efficiency. As we learned in the previous chapter, the evolution of AI towards General and Super Intelligence levels indicates a future where machines could perform tasks not only as humans do but potentially even more efficiently. However, the true frontier in this technological journey is instilling consciousness in AI – endowing machines with self-awareness and an understanding of their existence.

If we could infuse AI with a consciousness akin to human beings, we would be on the brink of a groundbreaking revelation. Such a development would blur the lines between human and machine, leading us to question the very essence of sentience. In this scenario, AI would transcend its role as a mere tool and emerge as an entity capable of introspection, emotion, and independent thought.

This brings us to a captivating hypothesis: if humans are akin to biological machines, could it be that we, too, are the creation of a higher intelligence? The idea that humans are programmed by a supremely intelligent being – whom many cultures and philosophies identify as God – opens a region of philosophical and existential inquiry. It suggests that our consciousness and self-awareness, much like what we aspire to create in AI, might be the result of a divine design.

Are we, in our essence, programmed entities in a grand design, or are we something more? As we navigate these questions, we tread a path that intertwines technology, philosophy, and spirituality, leading us closer to understanding the nature of consciousness and the possible existence of a cosmic architect.

The Essence of Being: Human Consciousness vs. AI Awareness

At the heart of this exploration is the concept of consciousness. Humans, as biological entities, exhibit a level of consciousness that is characterized by self-awareness, perception, and complex emotional capacities. This consciousness is not just a byproduct of our biological makeup; it is the essence of our experience and interaction with the world. In contrast, current AI systems, while advanced in processing and decision-making, lack this fundamental aspect of consciousness. They operate on logic and data, devoid of the subjective experience that characterizes human consciousness.

However, the future of AI promises a transformation. As we venture into the field of Artificial General Intelligence and beyond, we are not just looking at machines that can mimic human tasks, but at the potential for these machines to develop a form of consciousness. The question then arises: can AI ever truly become conscious in the way humans are, or will it be a different kind of awareness, unique to the synthetic nature of machines?

From the intricate workings of the brain, often compared to a supercomputer, to the complex biochemical processes that sustain life, we find an incredible level of sophistication that rivals, and in many ways, surpasses our best technological creations. This biological machinery is self-healing, self-replicating, and capable of learning - traits we aspire to emulate in AI.

We are at the brink of a new era in both technology and philosophy, where the lines between life and machine are not just blurred but intertwined. This exploration is more than scientific; it is a journey into the heart of what it means to exist and to be aware.

The journey to understand consciousness, whether embodied in flesh or manifested in silicon, takes us to the very core of what it means to be alive. This exploration transcends the physical boundaries of existence, probing into the province of awareness, experience, and self-perception.

Consider, for instance, the phenomenon of dreaming. In our dreams, we experience a reality that is entirely our own, created by our subconscious mind. Our brain, a biological marvel, conjures up vivid landscapes, complex narratives, and intense emotions, all while our conscious self is at rest. This ability to generate a conscious experience, even in sleep, offers a profound insight into what it means to be alive and aware.

Now, let's juxtapose this with the burgeoning field of AI. Imagine an advanced AI system designed to simulate human dreams. This AI would analyze vast amounts of data on human dreaming patterns, narratives, and emotional responses to generate its own 'dreams.' But can these simulated dreams, products of algorithms and data processing, be equated with the human experience of dreaming? Does the ability to replicate the mechanics of dreaming in silicon confer upon AI a form of consciousness akin to human experience?

This comparison opens up a myriad of philosophical questions. It challenges us to define the essence of consciousness. Is it the mere processing of information and generation of responses, or is it something more intangible, something inherently tied to the organic experience of life?

Moreover, the pursuit of understanding consciousness in AI prompts us to reevaluate our own consciousness. If a machine can replicate functions of the human mind, what does that reveal about our understanding of the mind itself? Are our thoughts, dreams, and emotions purely the result of complex biological processes, or is there an element of our consciousness that is beyond the scope of what can be replicated in silicon?

In seeking a deeper understanding of consciousness, we find ourselves at the intersection of technology, psychology, and philosophy. This journey is not just about understanding AI; it's about simplifying the mysteries of the human mind and the essence of what it means to be truly alive and aware.

As we progress through this exploration of consciousness and the nature of being, both in humans and potential AI, it's important to recognize that our current understanding is just the beginning. In upcoming chapters, we will explore the intricacies of the human mind and consciousness, particularly after exploring the expansive concept of the Metaverse and the role of avatars within it. The insights gained from understanding these digital spheres will offer us a unique perspective on our own existence as biological machines.

The content you've encountered so far serves as an initial foundation, a preliminary framework for a more profound exploration. It's designed to prepare you for a deeper dive into how we, as humans, might be intricately designed and programmed by a higher intelligence, often referred to as God. This exploration is not just about understanding the mechanics of our existence but also about appreciating the complexity and sophistication with which we have been created.

In the subsequent chapters, where we examine the Metaverse and the concept of avatars, we will revisit the topic of human consciousness and our parallels with AI. This revisit will be enriched with new insights and perspectives gained from our journey through virtual worlds and digital identities.

Ultimately, the journey through this book is not just a adventure for knowledge but a pursuit of understanding our place in the grand design, possibly orchestrated by a divine creator. Each chapter builds upon the last, weaving together technology, spirituality, and philosophy to form a comprehensive view of our existence and the potential future of AI. So, as we venture forward, keep in mind that what we've explored so far is just the beginning, and there is much more to uncover about the fascinating nature of our reality.

Chapter 05

The Anatomy of the Metaverse: Dissecting Virtual Realities

Throughout our journey thus far, we have explored into the complex mechanics of AI and contemplated the intriguing concept that humans may essentially be akin to biological machines. These sophisticated organic entities, as I have suggested, could potentially be the creation of a higher intelligence, a being we commonly call God. At this juncture, I encourage you to take a moment and consider this significant parallel: the prospect of endowing AI machines with a type of consciousness similar to human beings, and the captivating idea that we, too, might be entities crafted with deliberate programming.

The key to this parallel lies in unfolding the enigma of consciousness. If we can decode this elusive concept, we might bridge the gap between synthetic AI and organic human experience. This exploration, however, is vast and complex, and I plan to revisit and understand deeper into it in subsequent chapters. Before we venture further into the orbit of consciousness, let us turn our attention to another concept: the Metaverse.

Understanding the Metaverse is pivotal in our journey. It's not just a digital universe; it's a microcosm that mirrors the vast, possibly designed universe we inhabit. The Metaverse, a collective virtual shared space, is created by the convergence of enhanced physical reality and persistent virtual spaces. It's a region where avatars represent us, where digital economies thrive, and where social interactions transcend physical boundaries.

As we explore the Metaverse, consider it as a model, a smaller scale representation of how our universe might have been designed. The rules, the interactions, the very fabric of the Metaverse might offer us insights into the larger workings of our cosmos. Could our universe be, in a sense, a grand-scale Metaverse, programmed and designed with laws and parameters by a higher intelligence?

In this chapter, we will explore the Metaverse not just as a digital phenomenon, but as a key to understanding the potential design and programming of our universe. We'll look at how this digital cosmo functions, its parallels with our physical world, and what it can teach us about creation, existence, and the possibility of a divinely crafted universe.

By understanding the Metaverse, we might find clues to some of the most profound questions: How was our universe designed? What rules govern its functioning? Are we, like avatars in the Metaverse, representations of something greater in a vast, cosmic scheme?

The concept of Metaverse

For those just beginning to explore the concept of the Metaverse, a good starting point is to dive into some online resources. I recommend browsing the internet and watching videos to get a feel for what virtual worlds are like. These digital spheres are often best represented in media that visually capture their expansive and immersive nature.

If you've ever had the opportunity to experience a virtual world through VR (Virtual Reality) glasses, you'll find it easier to grasp the idea of the Metaverse. VR technology offers a glimpse into what the Metaverse embodies - a fully immersive, 3D environment where interaction feels as real as it does in the physical world. In VR, you can move, explore, and interact in ways that closely mirror real-life experiences, which is essentially what the Metaverse aims to achieve on a much grander scale.

The Metaverse extends this concept by creating a persistent, ever-evolving virtual space that exists parallel to our physical reality. It's a place where digital interactions aren't just limited to single sessions or experiences but are part of a larger, continuous digital existence.

So, if the Metaverse is a new concept for you, think of it as an extension of the virtual reality experiences you might already be familiar with, but on a much larger and more complex scale.

The Metaverse can be thought of as a vast, virtual world, much like the internet, but more immersive and interactive. Imagine putting on a pair of special glasses (like VR headsets) and suddenly finding yourself in a 3D world where you can walk around, meet people, attend events, play games, and even shop, just like you do in the real world. In the Metaverse, you have an avatar, a digital version of yourself, which you can customize to look however you want.

It's like a combination of a video game, a virtual reality experience, and the internet all rolled into one. You can interact with other people's avatars, just like interacting with people in real life, but through a digital medium.

Crafting Virtual Worlds: The Metaverse Through Unity and Unreal

This part of our exploration will particularly resonate with programmers and developers who have dabbled in creating applications using platforms like Unity or Unreal Engine. Just as these tools allow us to construct complex virtual environments from scratch, they offer a compelling analogy for how one might imagine the creation of our universe.

When we begin building an application in a platform like Unity, the first step is akin to a divine act of creation – we start by adding land to what was once empty space. This virtual land forms the foundation of our digital sphere, much like the celestial bodies that constitute the physical universe.

Then comes a critical component – gravity. In our virtual world, we introduce gravity to anchor objects and give them weight, just as in the universe, gravity governs the motion of planets and stars. This addition transforms our digital space from a mere visual spectacle to an interactive environment.

Next, we introduce an avatar. This digital entity, controlled by the user, is placed within the virtual world. The avatar's movement and interaction with the environment depend on the gravity we've programmed. It's fascinating to observe how the avatar navigates the terrain, jumps, or falls, all governed by the laws we've set in our virtual universe.

Drawing a parallel to the creation of our universe, one might ponder if a similar process was involved. Could it be that a higher intelligence, much like a developer using Unity or Unreal, crafted the cosmos from an empty void, introduced laws like gravity, and then populated it with living beings capable of movement and interaction?

This process, intricate and multi-layered, involves several key steps that transform a blank digital canvas into a vivid, interactive domain.

Conceptualization and Design: Every digital world begins with an idea. This stage is about conceptualizing the environment – envisioning the landscapes, the themes, the purpose, and the overall ambiance. Designers draft blueprints of the world, outlining its geography, architecture, and the rules that govern its physics and interactions.

Creating the Terrain: The next step is to sculpt the terrain of the digital world. Using specialized software, developers craft mountains, valleys, rivers, and plains, laying the groundwork for a rich, immersive environment. This terrain sets the stage for all subsequent elements of the world.

Implementing Physics and Mechanics: To make the world function realistically, or according to its intended design, physics engines are employed. These govern everything from gravity to the way light interacts with surfaces, giving the world a sense of realism and consistency.

Developing Ecosystems and Environments: This step involves populating the world with ecosystems, which could include flora, fauna, weather patterns, and environmental effects. This layer adds life to the world, making it dynamic and interactive.

Architecting Structures and Objects: Depending on the world's purpose, structures like buildings, bridges, and other objects are added. This is where the world gains complexity and depth, allowing for user interaction and exploration.

Character and Avatar Creation: Essential to any digital world are its inhabitants. Character creation involves designing the appearance, abilities, and behaviors of avatars and NPCs (Non-Playable Characters). This process often includes intricate modeling, texturing, and animation.

Scripting Narratives and Interactions: For worlds with a storyline, this phase involves scripting narratives, dialogues, and interaction pathways. It's about creating the plotlines and the choices that users will navigate, making the world not just a space but a story.

Integrating User Interface and Controls: A user interface is crucial for interaction. Developers integrate menus, control schemes, and interactive elements, ensuring that users can navigate and interact with the world seamlessly.

Releasing and Evolving: Once the digital world is introduced to users, it marks the start of an ever-evolving journey. The launch is just the beginning, not the end. To maintain the world's appeal and functionality, regular updates and maintenance are crucial. This continuous process of enhancement and refinement ensures that the virtual environment remains a lively and engaging space, evolving and adapting as time progresses.

Chapter 06

In Search of the Creator: Understanding Divinity in the Digital Cosmos

Throughout the previous chapters, we've explored the intricate dynamics of Artificial Intelligence and the Metaverse and their roles in our tangible world. Let's now extend this understanding to a hypothetical scenario where we craft a virtual universe that mirrors our own, complete with similar buildings, roads, and landscapes.

Imagine populating this digital universe with avatars that interact with their environment, consuming and utilizing virtual resources just as we do in the real world. The concept of programming such a universe and designing physical entities within it is within the world of possibility, especially considering the advancements in virtual reality and AI. As technology progresses, the idea of creating avatars that closely resemble real humans in appearance, behavior, and possibly thought, becomes increasingly feasible.

Now, picture these advanced avatars navigating the virtual world, engaging in daily activities, and interacting with their surroundings. The critical distinction between these digital beings and us lies in one fundamental aspect: consciousness. While these avatars can perform tasks and simulate human actions, they lack the self-awareness and consciousness that define human experience.

This idea leads us to a captivating hypothesis: What if our universe is comparable to this virtual sphere? Is it possible that we are similar to the avatars in our envisioned digital universe, crafted and positioned within a grand schema by a superior intelligence? Contemplating our existence as potentially crafted entities, rich with consciousness, invites us to reconsider the very fabric of our universe. This notion suggests that our reality might be more than a natural occurrence; it could be an elaborate construct, teeming with conscious beings, orchestrated by an unseen, higher power.

This comparison is not just about the visual or structural similarities, but also about the underlying principles and the roles played by inhabitants of these worlds – particularly avatars in the digital sphere.

To begin with, our physical world and a digitally created universe share fundamental attributes: spaces where entities interact, environments that adhere to specific rules, and a sense of continuity and presence. In both worlds, entities – whether humans or avatars – engage with their surroundings, forming relationships and impacting the ecosystem.

The creation of a digital universe often draws inspiration from the physical world. Designers and developers meticulously replicate landscapes, urban settings, and even natural laws to make these virtual worlds as lifelike as possible. This mirroring extends beyond mere aesthetics; it encompasses the dynamics of interaction, the physics of movement, and the simulation of natural phenomena like weather and light.

Avatars, the digital counterparts to humans in the virtual world, play a crucial role. They are more than just representations or digital puppets; they are the primary means through which users experience and influence the virtual world. In many ways, avatars are similar to us in their capacity to interact, perceive, and partake in the digital environment.

The God-like Role of a Developer

In this imaginative exploration, I step into the role of a virtual world architect. Envision a digital universe meticulously crafted by my hands – a universe replete with diverse landscapes, intricate buildings, and sentient avatars. Drawing from our discussions on the evolution of AI, particularly the advent of Artificial Super Intelligence, we venture into a scenario where these avatars are not just digital entities but conscious, self-aware beings, a feat achievable through the marvels of technological progress.

Let's imagine these avatars, human-like in appearance and consciousness, living in a simulation I have masterminded. They exist within the confines of this digital world, their lives unfolding under the rules of physics and dynamics that I, as their creator, have encoded. These immutable laws dictate their reality, setting the limits of their existence and experiences.

From the vantage point of these aware avatars, a profound question arises about their origin and the essence of their world. "Who is the architect of our universe?" they might ponder. In this digital dimension, the notion of 'God' becomes a tangible entity – the developer, in this case, myself.

It's an exploration that transcends mere philosophical musings, touching upon themes of creation, the essence of consciousness, and the interpretation of divinity in both our tangible world and the universe of the digital. As we unfold these themes, we gain deeper insights into the nature of existence. This journey is a reflection on our perpetual search to comprehend our place in the vast tapestry of the cosmos, whether as beings of flesh and blood or as creations of pixels and programming.

Chapter 07

Living in Illusion: Are We Residents of a Simulation?

In the previous chapter, we ventured into the creation of a digital universe imbued with consciousness. This exploration brings us to a thought-provoking possibility: Could our own reality be a simulation, intricately designed by a supremely intelligent entity? This entity, perhaps only conceivable within the bounds of our human cognition, might possess a complexity that stretches far beyond our imagination.

The idea that we might be living in a simulation presents a fascinating paradigm. In this scenario, much like the avatars in our digital universe, we could be entities within a meticulously crafted simulation, our existence and experiences defined by parameters set by an unseen creator. This creator, a being of immense intelligence and capability, could have designed the realities we navigate, the physical laws we adhere to, and the very essence of our perceived universe.

In this simulation, our world is akin to a programmed environment, a constructed reality where our choices, interactions, and perceptions are limited to what the simulation allows. Stepping beyond these boundaries might be impossible, much like an avatar attempting to transcend the digital confines of its world. The vast, unexplored darkness beyond our universe's observable limits could be the edge of our simulation, a boundary beyond which lies the unknown or the unfathomable.

Is everything we know and experience merely a part of a grand simulation, controlled and observed by a higher intelligence? Is our search for knowledge and understanding confined to the 'program' we exist within?

As we unpack the concept of living in a simulation, we not only question the nature of our reality but also examine the potential motivations and intentions of the hypothesized creator. This exploration is not just a scientific or philosophical inquiry; it's a journey into the heart of what it means to be human in a possibly preordained, simulated world.

As we continue to ponder the possibility of our universe being a grand simulation, let's consider the intriguing nature of light, a fundamental aspect of our cosmos. In a virtual simulator, we control the behavior of light and electricity to create realistic environments. Similarly, in our universe, light has a constant speed – a fundamental principle established by physics. Yet, the true nature of light remains one of the most enigmatic aspects of science.

Light exhibits dual characteristics – sometimes acting like a wave, and at other times, like a particle known as a photon. This duality, long a subject of scientific discourse, points to the complexity of understanding the universe's laws. What's particularly fascinating is how light seems to alter its behavior based on observation. When unobserved, it appears to behave as a wave, without a definite pattern or state. However, when we try to detect it, as in the famous double-slit experiment, it begins to behave like a particle.

This peculiar behavior of light might offer a glimpse into the nature of our reality if we consider the universe as a simulation. Everything around us could be an illusion, a play of light and energy, seamlessly operating in its natural state. Yet, the moment we direct our consciousness or apply scientific tools to observe and measure, these elements take on a definitive form and state.

In this book, while I steer clear of heavy scientific jargon, it is essential to highlight these aspects of light to underscore the complexity and, perhaps, the illusionary nature of our universe. This concept aligns intriguingly with the simulation hypothesis – that our reality might be a sophisticated construct, revealing its secrets only when probed by the observers within it, much like a programmed feature in a digital simulation.

Dreams of Creation: From Vishnu's Vision to Virtual Realities

In the fascinating world of Hindu mythology, there is an enthralling concept that the universe we inhabit is nothing but the dream of Vishnu, a prominent deity. This cosmic dream is said to be orchestrated by Brahma, another deity who plays the role of the creator. Interestingly, the entire lifespan of this universe is equivalent to just a single day in Brahma's existence. This notion paints the universe not as a random occurrence but as a divine imagination's manifestation, propelling us into the concept of the Multiverse – a universe of limitless possibilities and numerous parallel realities.

This mythological view of the universe as a divine dream opens up intriguing parallels to our modern-day explorations of virtual worlds. In the context of the previous chapter, where I described the creation of a digital universe, the comparison becomes even more vivid. In this digital sphere, governed by my own designs and rules, I embody a role similar to that of Brahma, the creator. This act of crafting a virtual universe can be seen as a modern parallel to the ancient mythological act of creation.

Taking this analogy further, consider the scenario where multiple developers, each with their unique vision and creativity, take up creating their digital universes. This situation mirrors the concept of multiple creators, each giving life to a distinct universe within the vast Multiverse. Alternatively, one could imagine a scenario where a universe is programmed to replicate itself, spawning countless versions, each a variant of the original. Such replicas could present diverse possibilities and experiences for the avatars inhabiting them, encapsulating the essence of a Multiverse.

This idea of the Multiverse, as posited in Hindu mythology and mirrored in our digital creations, suggests that our perceived reality might be one of many such manifestations. Each universe, whether a product of divine dream or digital programming, represents a unique creation borne out of imagination and creativity.

As we go deeper into this book, particularly when exploring the concept of God, we will revisit and expand upon this notion. We will explore how the idea of a creator, be it in the domain of mythology or virtual realities, influences our understanding of existence. The concept of a Multiverse not only broadens our perception of reality but also opens up avenues to ponder the limitless possibilities that might exist beyond our current comprehension.

In addition to the idea of multiple creators or universes, the concept of a Multiverse challenges our traditional understanding of time, space, and existence. It invites us to consider the possibility that what we perceive as reality is merely one version of many possible realities. This perspective encourages us to question the nature of our existence and the universe we live in. Are we, like the avatars in a digital cosmo, simply inhabitants of a much larger and more complex cosmic design?

This exploration into the Multiverse concept also touches upon the philosophical and scientific implications of such a theory. From a philosophical standpoint, it offers a new way of looking at existential questions about the purpose and nature of life. Scientifically, it aligns with some interpretations of quantum mechanics and theories in cosmology that suggest the existence of parallel universes or alternate dimensions.

Moreover, the idea of the universe as a dream or a carefully crafted simulation raises profound questions about consciousness and reality. What is the nature of consciousness in such a universe? Are we, as conscious beings, experiencing a reality that is shaped and defined by a higher intelligence, much like the avatars in a virtual world are governed by their programmer?

As we explore these questions, we begin to see the parallels between ancient mythologies and modern scientific theories. Both seek to explain the nature of the universe and our place within it, albeit in different languages and frameworks. The mythological concept of the Multiverse and the modern idea of a simulated reality represent two sides of the same coin – attempts to understand the unfathomable complexity and wonder of the cosmos.

Chapter 08

Deciphering the Cosmic Code: Understanding the Eternal Laws of the Universe

Throughout the earlier chapters of this book, we've ventured into the concept of creating simulated worlds, akin to our own universe. Yet, it's pivotal to acknowledge that the fabrication of a universe resembling ours demands a technological prowess and creative vision far beyond our current capabilities. This becomes evident when we dig into the atomic level – consider the immense computational power required to simulate just one spin of an electron around an atom. It's estimated that simulating such a spin could require around 50 GB of memory. Now, imagine the colossal number of spins and interactions happening at the atomic level across the entire universe. The sheer scale is staggering, underscoring the complexity and sophistication of a force capable of creating and maintaining such a system.

Our journey through the previous chapters aimed to draw parallels between our technological advancements and a God-like capacity for creation. This comparison serves as a lens through which we can begin to conceptualize the idea of a higher power – a God. However, to truly appreciate the eternal laws that govern our universe, we must plumb deeper into the fundamental questions that have intrigued humanity for ages.

At the heart of these eternal laws lies the concept of order amidst chaos. The universe, in all its vastness and complexity, operates on principles that maintain a delicate balance. These laws, from gravity to electromagnetism, quantum mechanics to relativity, all work in concert to sustain the cosmos. They are the unseen rules that dictate the motion of planets, the fusion in stars, the dance of galaxies, and the very fabric of spacetime.

To understand these laws, we must first consider the fundamental forces of nature. These forces–gravitational, electromagnetic, strong nuclear, and weak nuclear – are the pillars upon which the universe stands. Each force plays a unique role: gravity keeps planets in orbit, electromagnetism allows for the formation of atoms and molecules, and the nuclear forces govern the heart of stars and the subtleties of subatomic particles.

Another aspect of these eternal laws is the principle of cause and effect, often encapsulated in the concept of karma in various philosophies. It suggests that every action in the universe leads to a corresponding reaction, maintaining a cosmic equilibrium. This principle is not just a spiritual or philosophical concept but is mirrored in the laws of physics, such as Newton's third law of motion.

Furthermore, the second law of thermodynamics, which addresses the concept of entropy, provides insight into the nature of order and disorder in the universe. It states that in a closed system, entropy, or disorder, tends to increase over time. This law gives us a glimpse into the fate of the universe and the inexorable march towards a state of maximum entropy.

The beauty of these cosmic laws lies in their universality and consistency. They do not waver or discriminate; they apply equally to a speck of dust as they do to a colossal galaxy. It's this consistency that has allowed scientists to make groundbreaking discoveries and to predict celestial phenomena with remarkable precision.

Our exploration into these laws also touches upon the most significant and enduring questions of our existence: the origin of the universe, the nature of time and space, and the ultimate fate of all cosmic matter. The Big Bang theory, the concept of spacetime curvature in General Relativity, and the mysterious dark matter and dark energy – all these ideas form part of our hunt to decode the universe's eternal laws.

In conclusion, as we navigate through these profound and complex concepts, we gain not just scientific knowledge but also a deeper appreciation for the intricacy and majesty of the universe. This journey is a testament to human curiosity and our undying search to understand the cosmos. It reminds us that while we may draw parallels between our technology and divine-like powers, the true nature of the universe's eternal laws is a puzzle that continues to challenge and inspire us.

Chapter 09

Contemplating the Divine: Who is God?

In your pursuit to grasp the true nature of God, have you stumbled upon an unequivocal and precise explanation? Time and again, conventional religious texts and spiritual mentors envelop this inquiry in a veil of obscurity, resulting in more confusion than clarity. Presenting this apparently simple question frequently elicits a dissection of the query rather than a direct answer, spiraling into a maze of philosophical discourse. Such reactions can sometimes be perceived as an outright defiance of the existence of a supreme power.

Yet, if we approach this subject with a logical and inquisitive mindset, isn't questioning an essential part of our journey to understanding? Many believe that a higher power has bestowed us with intellect and consciousness. Therefore, isn't it our right, perhaps even our obligation, to seek clarity about this divine entity?

This chapter is a deep dive into the complexities surrounding the idea of God. It's an exploration that seeks to untangle the often conflicting narratives offered by diverse belief systems and doctrines. Employing our inherent faculties of logic and reflection, we strive to decode the concept of a creator, a supreme entity, or a universal intelligence. This exploration isn't about challenging faith or belief; instead, it's about seeking a more profound, nuanced comprehension of what or who God might be, beyond the constraints of conventional teachings and interpretations.

Throughout history, humanity's relationship with the divine has been complex and multifaceted. In some cultures, God is seen as a singular, all-powerful being who watches over the universe. In others, God takes on many forms, each representing different aspects of the divine. Some philosophical traditions even question the need for a personal deity, suggesting that the divine might be an impersonal force or a fundamental quality of the universe.

The nature of God has also been a central topic in various philosophical debates. From the ancient Greeks pondering the first cause to modern thinkers questioning the role of God in a world governed by scientific laws, the concept of a supreme being has been analyzed, debated, and reinterpreted in countless ways.

Furthermore, the chapter examines the role of faith in understanding God. For many, faith is a bridge between the known and the unknown, a way to connect with a higher power beyond the limits of human understanding. Yet, others argue that faith should go hand in hand with reason, allowing us to question and understand our beliefs critically.

We also explore the impact of scientific understanding on our perception of God. In an age where science provides explanations for many phenomena once attributed to divine intervention, how does our image of God change? Does science diminish the need for God, or does it offer a different way of understanding the divine?

This in-depth exploration aims to provide a space for reflection and understanding, inviting readers to ponder their beliefs and the nature of the divine. Whether you are a person of faith, a skeptic, or somewhere in between, this chapter offers a thoughtful examination of one of humanity's most enduring questions: Who, or what, is God?

And the Clear Answer is…

The Creator of this Universe is not "God"

We have ventured through the idea that our existence might be part of a simulated reality, intricately designed and governed by a set of precise, immutable laws – the eternal laws of the universe. This creator, the architect of our cosmos, is undoubtedly a being of immense intelligence, existing beyond the constraints of time and space, untouched by the laws of physics as we understand them. Yet, this raises a profound question: if this creator is God, then who created this God? It's a paradox that has puzzled thinkers, theologians, and philosophers for centuries.

To address this conundrum, we must first explore the concept of God as traditionally understood in various cultures and religions. In many belief systems, God is seen as the ultimate creator, an omnipotent and omniscient entity responsible for the creation and maintenance of the universe. However, this traditional view of God often leads to the logical dilemma of the 'first cause' – if everything has a creator, then who created God?

This question leads us to consider the possibility that the term 'God' might not adequately describe the creator of our universe. Perhaps, this entity, this supreme architect, is something beyond our current understanding, beyond even the traditional definitions of divinity. It may be more apt to view this entity not as God but as a profoundly advanced intelligence, existing in a world beyond our comprehension.

In Hindu mythology, the concept of God

is multifaceted and complex. Indra, the king of gods, when questioned by Hemavathi about the true nature of God, found himself unable to grasp or explain this infinite entity. This story reflects the limitations of even the most powerful beings in understanding the true essence of the creator. It suggests that the actual nature of God, or the ultimate creator, is an infinite, eternal mystery, unfathomable by our physical minds.

Even within our simulated universe hypothesis, the entity we refer to as the creator – the one who designed and programmed our reality – may itself be a creation of a higher intelligence. This perspective aligns with the concept of a hierarchy of creators, each level transcending the understanding of the one below it.

As we probe deeper into this topic, we explore various philosophical and theological perspectives on the nature of the creator. We examine the arguments put forth by different schools of thought, from those that posit an uncaused, self-existing creator to those that suggest an infinite regress of creators.

Furthermore, this chapter inquires into the scientific perspective on the universe's creation. The Big Bang theory, the most widely accepted scientific explanation of the universe's origin, describes a singular beginning. Yet, it leaves unanswered questions about what preceded the Big Bang or what exists outside the observable universe. These scientific mysteries add another layer to our understanding of the universe's creation.

In addition to philosophical and scientific explorations, we also consider the spiritual and existential implications of this discussion. If the creator of our universe is not the ultimate God, what does this mean for our understanding of purpose, destiny, and our place in the cosmos? How does this impact our spiritual beliefs and practices?

Throughout history, humans have sought to understand their origins and the nature of their existence. This exploration has led to the creation of myths, religions, and scientific theories, each attempting to provide answers to these fundamental questions.

I repeat, this journey is not just about seeking answers but about embracing the mysteries of our existence and the infinite possibilities that lie beyond our current understanding.

The Divine Mathematics: Interpreting God Through Zero and Nine

In the journey to comprehend the concept of God, an intriguing approach is to explore it through the lens of two fundamental numbers: zero and nine. These numbers, in their simplicity, embody profound philosophical and spiritual significance. Zero represents the concept of nothingness, the void from which all existence springs, while nine symbolizes completeness, the ultimate end of a numerical journey.

At the outset, zero is a symbol of the void, the absence of everything. It is the starting point, a state of pure potentiality where all creation begins. In many spiritual traditions, this nothingness is akin to the formless, boundless nature of the divine – the source from which all existence emerges. Zero, in its essence, represents the unmanifested, the unseen force that underpins all creation.

Conversely, nine is seen as the number of completion, the finality of the numerical sequence. In mathematics, the unique properties of nine are fascinating – any number multiplied by nine reduces back to nine when its digits are added together. This property of nine, known as its 'digital root,' reflects a sense of returning to the source, a cycle of going out into the world and coming back to the origin.

The interplay between zero and nine is akin to the dance of creation and dissolution in the universe. Zero symbolizes the unmanifested divine, the source of all potential, while nine represents the manifested universe in all its complexity and completeness. This dual nature mirrors the concept of God as both the creator and the sustainer of the universe.

Moreover, the mathematical operations involving zero and nine reveal deeper spiritual truths. Multiplying any number with zero results in zero, illustrating the idea that merging with the divine void leads to the dissolution of individual identity. On the other hand, dividing any number by zero results in infinity, signifying the boundless, infinite nature of the divine.

Adding zero to any number does not alter its value, symbolizing the idea that the divine presence, like zero, is omnipresent yet does not interfere with the individual essence of beings. Similarly, adding nine to a number and calculating its digital root brings us back to the original number, reflecting the idea that all creation, despite its apparent diversity, ultimately returns to its singular divine source.

In Hinduism, for instance, the concept of 'Shunya,' representing the void, is a key aspect of understanding the nature of reality and consciousness. In Kabbalistic traditions, the sefirot, or emanations of God, are often counted as ten, with the first being the unknowable divine essence, akin to zero.

We also examine the role of numbers in different cultures and their symbolic meanings in understanding the universe and the divine. From the mystical significance of numbers in Pythagorean philosophy to their use in modern science to decipher the laws of the universe, numbers have always been a bridge between the material and the spiritual.

In addition to philosophical and cultural perspectives, the chapter explores the scientific implications of these concepts. The idea of zero and infinity plays a crucial role in modern physics and cosmology, shaping our understanding of the universe's origin, structure, and ultimate fate.

Recognizing the omnipresence of the divine, symbolized by zero, and the completeness of existence, symbolized by nine, can transform our perspective on life, relationships, and our place in the universe.

The Contemplation of Prayer: Should we pray?

In pondering the question, "Should we pray?" I find myself delving into a profound aspect of human existence. This question is not merely about the act of praying but about our connection to the cosmos and its creator. As I reflect on this, I share my thoughts, drawn not just from spiritual texts or philosophical musings, but from the deep well of personal experience and introspection.

Firstly, it's important to acknowledge the universal laws set forth by the creator of this universe. These laws, as I understand them, are the fundamental principles that govern existence. Within this framework, prayer can be seen as a way of aligning ourselves with these cosmic laws. When prayers are offered from the heart, with sincerity and depth of feeling, they resonate with these universal principles. Such prayers, I believe, have the potential to reach the creator.

However, prayer, when performed out of fear, obligation, or without genuine realization, loses its essence. In such cases, it might be better not to pray at all. This perspective might seem controversial or unconventional, especially in a world where prayer is often seen as a religious duty or a means to seek divine favor. But my understanding, shaped by years of contemplation and personal experiences, suggests that the value of prayer lies in its authenticity and alignment with one's true self and the larger cosmic order.

I want to emphasize that whether you choose to pray or not does not significantly impact the creator. The universe operates on principles that are independent of individual acts of worship. Life, in all its complexity and beauty, continues regardless of our personal devotions. This understanding is rooted in the core function of karma, a concept I explored in depth in my previous chapter "Karma: Unveiling Its Essence in the Cosmic Scheme."

Consider the simple yet profound example of observing animals or insects, such as dogs or ants. They typically don't catch our attention unless they do something out of the ordinary. Our response to them is contingent upon their actions. Similarly, the creator has set certain laws in motion, creating a universe that functions autonomously, much like a self-sustaining ecosystem.

This does not diminish the value of prayer but rather redefines it. Prayer, in this context, is not a transactional act but a means of personal growth, reflection, and alignment with the cosmic laws. It's a tool for internal exploration, for connecting with the deeper aspects of our being, and for harmonizing with the universe's rhythm.

The concept of prayer as a form of meditation or mindfulness practice become a way of centering oneself, of finding peace and clarity amidst life's chaos. It's a practice that transcends religious boundaries, offering a universal pathway to inner tranquility and wisdom.

We also explore the idea of prayer as a means of expressing gratitude, love, and compassion. In this perspective, prayer is not just about asking for help or favors but about acknowledging the beauty and bounty of life, about connecting with others and the universe in a spirit of thankfulness and kindness.

We address the skepticism and questions that many people, including myself, have faced regarding the efficacy and purpose of prayer. Through this exploration, we discover that prayer, in its truest form, is not about altering the course of events or seeking divine intervention but about finding our place in the cosmic scheme, about understanding ourselves and our connection to the universe. Prayer, in this sense, becomes a journey of self-discovery and alignment with the eternal laws of existence.

The Universe as Our Ultimate Guide: Redefining the Concept of Guru

I want to dig into a topic that has long been a subject of contemplation and debate – the concept of a Guru, or spiritual teacher. The assertion that one cannot reach God without a Guru is a common theme in various spiritual traditions. However, through my journey and understanding, I have come to see this in a different light. We have often been misled by so-called gurus and misinterpretations of scriptures, leading to a convoluted understanding of spiritual guidance.

As discussed in my previous chapter, there's a distinction between the creator of the universe, the higher entity that we may refer to as God, and ourselves as human beings. Thus, we find ourselves in a cosmic triad: us as individuals, the universe's architect, and the ultimate divine source. Traditional scriptures state that attaining God is impossible without the guidance of a Guru. I propose that the true Guru, in this cosmic scheme, is the universe itself, created by the architect. The key to connecting with this cosmic mentor lies in adhering to the universal laws.

The search for spiritual enlightenment often leads people to seek external Gurus – figures revered in various religions as masters or mentors. Each religious tradition presents its own interpretation of God, shaped by cultural beliefs and individual experiences. In this pursuit, the essential teaching is frequently lost: the universe, in all its grandeur and complexity, is our true guide.

The universe as a Guru is an expansive, all-encompassing teacher that instructs through the laws of nature, the rhythms of life, and the intricate tapestry of existence.

Unlike human gurus, the universe does not offer dogmatic teachings or rigid doctrines. Instead, it imparts wisdom through experience, observation, and the innate understanding that comes from being a part of this vast cosmic play.

To truly connect with this universal Guru, we must attune ourselves to its laws – the principles that govern everything from the smallest particle to the largest galaxy. These laws are not written texts or spoken words but are found in the harmony of nature, the patterns of the cosmos, and the depths of our consciousness.

One of the profound lessons the universe teaches us is interconnectedness. Everything in the cosmos is interlinked, from the stars in the sky to the cells in our bodies. This interconnectedness reminds us that our actions and thoughts have far-reaching consequences, resonating through the web of existence. Understanding this interconnectedness deepens our sense of responsibility and empathy, guiding us towards more harmonious living.

Another vital lesson is the impermanence of life. The universe is in a constant state of flux, with stars being born and dying, seasons changing, and life evolving. This impermanence teaches us to embrace change, to let go of attachments, and to appreciate the transient beauty of life.

Additionally, the universe instructs us in the art of balance. Just as the cosmos maintains a delicate equilibrium, we too are encouraged to find balance in our lives – between action and rest, giving and receiving, growth and preservation.

We examine the role of human Gurus, the value they have added to individual spiritual journeys, and the potential pitfalls of blindly following a human teacher.

This perspective encourages a more holistic approach to spirituality, integrating aspects of science, philosophy, and personal experience. By recognizing the universe as our ultimate Guru, we open ourselves to a profound source of wisdom, drawing lessons from the very fabric of existence and our place within it. This understanding is not just a philosophical concept but a practical guide for living a more aware, connected, and fulfilling life.

Rethinking the Renunciation: Should We Forsake the Material World?

Let me tell you a story that mirrors the quandary faced by many in their spiritual journey. This tale encapsulates the struggle of an individual torn between the allure of material existence and the pursuit of spiritual enlightenment. It serves as a reflection of the complex dance between the world we see and the unseen provinces of spiritual consciousness.

Our protagonist is a person deeply influenced by a myriad of spiritual gurus and revered texts. Each source resonates with a unanimous message – the world is an illusion. This profound yet perplexing teaching sends him into a spiral of deep confusion and introspection. In his earnest inquiry for spiritual clarity, he begins a series of drastic life changes.

His initial step is to cut off ties with friends, believing that solitude will lead him closer to spiritual truth. Yet, this step only deepens his sense of isolation, failing to bring the inner peace he yearns for. He then leaves his job, thinking that shedding professional responsibilities will simplify his path to enlightenment. However, this too does not quell his inner turmoil. The journey takes a more austere turn as he severely restricts his diet, only to find his physical and mental health deteriorating.

In a final, desperate attempt to escape the 'illusions' of the world, he leaves his family, convinced that their presence impedes his spiritual progress. He retreats to the solitude of the mountains, hoping to find in nature the answers that eluded him in human connections.

Two years pass in this self-imposed exile. One day, a letter arrives from his brother, expressing concern and affection, accompanied by flowers. His response, sent back through a simple post mail, is both poignant and revealing: 'Yes, I am all fine. Now I can control things. And the flowers were tasty.' This reply, in its oddity, lays bare the irony of his situation. In seeking control and enlightenment, he has become disconnected from the fundamental human experiences of love, relationship, and community.

This story is a microcosm of a dilemma that plagues many seekers. The belief that renunciation of the material world is the key to spiritual attainment is a pervasive one. However, as our protagonist's journey illustrates, this path often leads to more confusion and a sense of disconnection from the very essence of life. As I mentioned earlier from the creator's perspective, the physical world may be an illusion, but for us, it is the arena of our experiences and growth.

As we explore the importance of understanding and adhering to the universal laws that govern existence. These laws offer guidance on how to live a balanced and harmonious life, weaving together material responsibilities and spiritual pursuits. True spiritual growth involves confronting and understanding our deeper issues, not escaping from them.

Decoding Self-Awareness: A Personal Journey to Understanding

The concept of self-awareness is often clouded by misconceptions and misinterpretations. In my own journey of discovery and understanding, I have come to realize that self-awareness extends far beyond the orbits of introspection, meditation, or scrutinizing one's actions. It involves a profound realization and acknowledgment of our true essence and our place in the grand scheme of the universe.

When the topic of self-awareness arises, the typical response is to turn inwards, analyzing and judging our thoughts, actions, and motivations. This process, while beneficial in understanding our behaviors, only touches the surface of what true self-awareness entails. In my experience, genuine self-awareness is about recognizing that we are creations of a super-intelligent being and that our lives are guided by certain universal laws set by this creator. The essence of these laws is encapsulated in the concept of karma.

To understand self-awareness in this context, it is essential to dig deeper into what it means to be a creation of a higher intelligence. This recognition brings about a paradigm shift in how we view ourselves and our existence. It's a realization that we are not random products of chance but purposeful creations within a well-ordered cosmos.

In exploring the nature of the creator, we find that this super-intelligent entity has imbued the universe with a set of laws that govern everything – from the movements of celestial bodies to the workings of human lives. These laws are intricate, interconnected, and profoundly impactful. Understanding and aligning ourselves with these laws is a fundamental aspect of self-awareness.

At the heart of these universal laws is the concept of karma, a principle that emphasizes the cyclical nature of cause and effect. Every action, every thought, and every intention sets off a chain of reactions, shaping our experiences and our journey through life. Self-awareness, in this sense, is about recognizing the power and significance of our actions and their alignment with the cosmic order.

We also explore the role of consciousness in self-awareness. Consciousness, the awareness of one's own existence, thoughts, and surroundings, is a crucial component of self-awareness. It's through consciousness that we perceive ourselves and our relation to the universe. This relationship between self-awareness and consciousness is a complex and fascinating area that offers insights into the nature of human existence.

Understanding our true nature and the laws that govern our existence can transform our approach to life, relationships, and decision-making. It encourages us to live more mindfully, with greater empathy and a deeper sense of purpose.

In addition to the philosophical and practical aspects, we go into the scientific perspective on self-awareness. Modern psychology and neuroscience have made significant strides in understanding how self-awareness manifests in the human brain, providing a fascinating intersection between science and spirituality.

The Duality of Rest: Sleep Versus Meditation?

In the pursuit of understanding the complexities of human existence and the secrets of the universe, I often find myself contemplating the roles of sleep and meditation. These two states, while seemingly similar in their restorative functions, serve distinct purposes in our physical and spiritual journeys. In this chapter, I will explore the nuanced differences between sleep and meditation, and how they each contribute to our overall well-being and spiritual growth.

Let's begin by considering the human brain as a sophisticated computer, storing and processing vast amounts of data. Just like any advanced system, our brain accumulates 'cached' data – temporary information stored for quick access. Over time, this cache can become cluttered, necessitating a 'refresh' to clear out the unnecessary data and optimize performance. Sleep and meditation can be likened to this refresh command, each serving to rejuvenate the mind and body, albeit in different ways.

Sleep, an essential physiological process, is akin to the automatic refresh mode of a computer. It's a passive process where the body and mind undergo restoration and healing. During sleep, various biological processes occur, including the repair of cells and the consolidation of memories. Sleep provides a much-needed break from the sensory and cognitive stimuli of waking life, allowing the body to recharge and rejuvenate.

Meditation, on the other hand, is more akin to a manual refresh. It's an active process where we consciously direct our focus and attention. Unlike the passive state of sleep, meditation requires an active engagement of the mind. It's a practice of mindfulness, of being aware of our thoughts, emotions, and sensations without judgment. Meditation allows us to declutter our mental cache consciously, providing clarity and calmness.

The distinction between sleep and meditation lies in their approach to rejuvenation. Sleep rejuvenates us physically, providing the rest our bodies need to function optimally. Meditation, however, rejuvenates us mentally and spiritually. It enables us to clear our minds, gain insights into our thoughts and emotions, and connect with a deeper sense of self.

Now, addressing the question of whether sleep and meditation function in the same way, we encounter the duality of our existence as programmed by the universe's creator. Certain aspects of our being are refreshed during sleep – our physical bodies. Other aspects, particularly our consciousness and spiritual awareness, are rejuvenated through meditation. This distinction underscores the importance of both processes in our lives.

Moving to the broader question of whether meditation can lead to the attainment of God, as suggested by various scriptures, it's important to note that meditation is but one pathway among many. It's a tool that can aid in elevating our consciousness, in connecting with the higher aspects of our being. However, meditation alone is not the sole key to spiritual ascension.

The journey towards higher consciousness, towards understanding the divine or the creator, involves a multifaceted approach. It's a combination of meditation, ethical living, compassion, understanding the universal laws, and many other spiritual practices. Meditation is a crucial step on this journey, but it's part of a larger mosaic of spiritual growth. The balance between these two forms of rest is essential for holistic well-being. I invite readers to understand and appreciate the unique contributions of each practice to our well-being. By recognizing the importance of both physical rest and conscious mindfulness, we can begin on a more balanced and fulfilling journey towards self-discovery and spiritual growth.

The Genesis of Ultimate Truth: Death or Birth?

In the orbit of spiritual discourse, particularly within the Vedic scriptures and the teachings of various gurus, there's a common emphasis on death being the ultimate truth of existence. However, through my reflections and understanding, I have come to a different conclusion: the ultimate truth is not death, but birth. In this chapter, I will share my perspective on why I believe birth, rather than death, holds the key to understanding the profound mysteries of existence.

From my vantage point, death is an illusion, a transition rather than an end. Our physical form can be likened to a radio, meticulously programmed by the universe's creator to receive and interpret specific signals. This analogy extends to the idea that we are akin to robots, each encoded with a unique set of instructions that dictate our existence. In this cosmic design, the 'program' – the essence or soul of our being – transcends the physicality of our bodies, moving from one form to another in an eternal cycle of rebirth.

This concept of the soul's journey challenges the traditional view of death as the ultimate reality. Instead, it places birth at the center of the ultimate truth. Every being experiences birth; it is the universal constant in the cycle of existence. While our bodies are mortal, the soul within is perpetual, unbound by the physical constraints of death.

This understanding of birth as the fundamental truth of existence leads to intriguing possibilities about the nature of the soul and its journey. If we adhere to the universal laws set forth by the creator, it's conceivable that our souls are destined for greater purposes beyond our current existence. Perhaps, as we evolve spiritually, we are assigned higher responsibilities, maybe even the stewardship of other universes or dimensions.

The idea that one can ascend to higher levels of existence, taking on roles akin to creators or guardians of other spheres, is both exhilarating and humbling. It suggests a cosmic hierarchy where souls progress through various stages of development, each stage offering new opportunities for growth and service.

This perspective also ties into my previous discussion about the impossibility of comprehending 'God' in the traditional sense. If the creator of this universe has designed a system where the soul continually evolves, then understanding the true nature of God might be beyond our current scope. Our journey, then, is not about finding God in an absolute sense but about ascending through different levels of consciousness and responsibility. The realization that our physical existence is merely one phase in a much larger journey can transform our approach to life's challenges and joys.

From the philosophical standpoint, we explore concepts like reincarnation, the immortality of the soul, and the idea of a cosmic consciousness that connects all beings. From a scientific perspective, we examine theories in quantum physics and consciousness studies that might offer insights into the nature of the soul and its transmigration. If we view our current life as part of a larger journey of the soul, how does that change our approach to ethics, morality, and our responsibilities to each other and the planet?

I invite you to reconsider traditional views of death and to embrace a more expansive view of existence that transcends physical limitations. This exploration is not just about redefining our understanding of life and death; it is about recognizing our place in a grand cosmic scheme where birth is the genesis of an endless journey of growth, discovery, and elevation.

Religion's Role in the Cosmic Play

In my journey of understanding the universe and its intricacies, I have often pondered the role of religion. My conclusion might seem unconventional: I believe that the primary function of religion is to sow confusion. This perspective might be startling at first, but allow me to elaborate on why I view religion not as a beacon of clarity, but as an instrument in the cosmic play, possibly orchestrated by the creator of the universe to engage the inhabitants of the material world.

Religion, in my experience, often acts as a maze, with its complex doctrines, rituals, and teachings. While it claims to offer a path to understanding the divine, it frequently ends up entangling individuals in a web of confusion. As I've mentioned before, religions and their gurus tend to obfuscate rather than clarify the perspective of God, the individual, and the creator of the universe.

Consider this hypothetical scenario: I introduce a new term, "abcd," and declare it as a new religion. This religion amalgamates technological and spiritual perspectives to view God, thereby creating a unique framework of belief. Such an introduction would inevitably lead to the creation of a system that could challenge or even negate the teachings of existing religions. This example illustrates how religions can often diverge from understanding the true essence of the universe's creator.

In my view, the key to truly comprehending the creator's essence is not through religious doctrines but by following universal laws. These laws are not written in religious texts but are imprinted in the cosmos itself. They govern everything from the orbits of planets to the moral compass within each human being. Understanding and aligning ourselves with these laws is a personal journey, one that transcends religious boundaries and dogmas.

Religion may offer a sense of identity, community, and moral guidance. However, majorly it leads to divisiveness, dogmatism, and an external reliance for spiritual fulfillment. The psychological need for belonging and understanding can sometimes drive individuals to adhere rigidly to religious doctrines, overshadowing the personal journey of spiritual discovery. While religion has been a source of profound wisdom and ethical guidance for a few, but it has been extensively misused to propagate confusion, conflict, and division. The fine line between religious guidance and dogmatic rigidity is a crucial aspect of this discussion.

We also contemplate the idea of personal spirituality versus organized religion. Personal spirituality is an individual's unique connection with the universe, unmediated by religious doctrines or rituals. It's a direct, personal experience of the cosmic laws and the divine essence. This form of spirituality often provides a more authentic and unfiltered understanding of the universe and our place within it.

I propose you to reflect on their spiritual beliefs and practices, encouraging them to seek a personal connection with the cosmic laws rather than relying solely on religious doctrines. This exploration is not about discrediting religion but about recognizing its limitations and potential as one of many pathways in our journey of cosmic discovery. It's a journey that calls for introspection, openness, and a willingness to look beyond dogma to embrace a more personal and direct experience of the universe's profound mysteries.

The Enigma of Dreams

As I sit down to pen my thoughts on the enigmatic world of dreams, I must confess that I am still navigating through the fog of uncertainty about their true purpose. Dreams have always been a source of intrigue and wonder in my life, a nightly phenomenon that prompts more questions than answers. Through this chapter, I aim to share my personal reflections and experiences, delving into the elusive nature of dreams and their possible significance in our lives.

The principality of dreams, as I have come to understand, is not just a mere byproduct of our sleeping brains but a complex and mysterious world that may hold deeper meanings. In my own life, I have observed that dreams seem to be interwoven with our daily experiences and emotions, often reflecting our deepest fears, desires, and questions. It is as if, in our sleep, we enter a different dimension of existence where the subconscious mind takes over, presenting us with symbols and scenarios that are both baffling and enlightening.

My fascination with dreams began in my youth, and over the years, it has only grown stronger. I have experienced dreams that felt prophetic, dreams that seemed to offer solutions to problems I was facing, and dreams so surreal that they defied all logical explanation. These experiences have led me to believe that there is more to dreams than mere random neural activities during sleep.

I propose that dreams might be a mechanism, a subtle yet profound way through which the higher power or the universe communicates with us. This communication could be in the form of guidance, warnings, or even as a mirror reflecting our innermost thoughts and feelings. However, deciphering these messages is often a challenging task, as the language of dreams is symbolic and not always direct.

The interplay of divine messages with the neural networks of our brain adds another layer of complexity to dreams. It's as if these celestial hints get entangled with our cognitive processes, creating images and narratives that are sometimes clear, at other times cryptic. This fusion results in dreams being a unique blend of divine communication and personal psyche, a combination that is both fascinating and perplexing.

In my journey to understand dreams, I have often pondered their relationship with our daily lives. Are dreams merely reflections of our waking thoughts and emotions, or do they hold keys to deeper spiritual insights? My experiences have led me to lean towards the latter. Dreams, in my view, are not just passive experiences; they are active interactions with a deeper aspect of our existence.

This chapter is not an academic discourse on dreams but a personal narrative exploring their mystery and allure. Here, I share stories of dreams that have left a lasting impact on my life, dreams that have guided me, confused me, and sometimes, transformed me. Each dream I recount is a piece in the puzzle of understanding the role and purpose of dreams in our lives.

In sharing these experiences, I also probe the emotional and psychological impact of dreams. How do they shape our feelings, influence our decisions, and affect our waking life? I explore the aftereffects of particularly vivid or disturbing dreams and how they sometimes blur the lines between reality and illusion.

As I continue to explore the world of dreams, I'm drawn to a fascinating hypothesis: could it be that we, as creations of a higher power, possess an innate ability to create universes within our dreams? This notion resonates intriguingly with the idea found in Hindu mythology, where it's said we exist within Vishnu's dream. In my dreams, am I not, in some way, akin to Vishnu, weaving together my own universe?

Consider this: each night, as I sleep, the span of my dreams could very well encompass the entire existence of a universe. This concept transforms my understanding of dreaming. It's not merely a sequence of images or narratives; it's an act of creation. Each dream is potentially a complex, self-contained universe, with its unique laws, entities, and timelines.

This perspective leads me to ponder the infinite loop of creation. In our dreams, do we become creators like Vishnu, spinning out universes while ourselves existing within a cosmic dream? This concept offers a multi-layered view of reality, where each dream is a thread in a vast cosmic tapestry, each potentially birthing countless realities.

By embracing this idea, I begin to see dreaming not just as a subconscious activity but as an essential cosmic function. Each dream, in its way, is akin to a deity's act of creation. It suggests that we, in our capacity to dream, participate in the ongoing cycle of creation, each night weaving new realities in a cosmic play.

As I explore this further, I consider the implications of being a creator in my sleep. If my dreams are indeed universes, what does that reveal about my potential in the waking world? Could my nocturnal adventures hold lessons or insights about my waking life?

The potential cosmic significance of dreams thus sheds new light on their role. They are not just psychologically significant but cosmically vital. Dreams elevate from being a mere nighttime escape to being pivotal in the universe's ongoing creation and maintenance.

I want you to reimagine the nature of dreams. They are more than mere subconscious processes; they are manifestations of our inherent creative powers, our intimate connection to the universe.

The Dilemma of Meat Consumption

As I address the topic of whether to consume meat or not, I approach it not from a standpoint of religious dogma, but through a lens of consciousness, emotions, and their subtle energies. In various conversations and debates I've encountered, meat consumption is often linked with the law of karma – the principle of cause and effect. The common argument is that harming an animal leads to negative consequences for the perpetrator. However, my understanding of this issue probes deeper, extending into the realms of consciousness and emotional energy.

In my earlier discussions about how the universe operates on the principles of consciousness and emotional waves, I've come to appreciate the significance of these forces in our daily lives. When we consider the act of killing an animal for food, it's not just a physical act; it's an event that releases a cascade of emotions and energies. Animals, like humans, experience fear and aggression. When an animal is slaughtered, especially when it's not a natural death, these emotions – fear or aggression – are released into the environment, albeit in a form invisible to the naked eye.

Observing people's behaviors and temperaments has led me to a compelling hypothesis: individuals who consume excessive amounts of meat often exhibit heightened levels of aggression or fear. This pattern suggests that the emotional energy released at the time of the animal's death doesn't just dissipate; it finds a way to manifest, influencing those who consume the meat. It's as if the fear or aggression of the animal becomes a part of those who partake in eating its flesh.

This perspective on meat consumption invites us to consider the broader implications of our dietary choices. It's not merely about nutrition or personal preference; it's about the interconnectedness of all living beings and the transfer of energy that occurs in the act of eating.

Moreover, this view aligns with the concept that our choices, including our dietary ones, have ripple effects that extend beyond the immediate physical outcomes. They touch upon the ethical, emotional, and energetic realms. The decision to consume meat, therefore, becomes a question of aligning our actions with the principles of compassion, empathy, and awareness.

Nonetheless, as I've previously noted, categorizing things as strictly good or bad is often an oversimplification. Instead, I offer this as a logical perspective to consider.

Understanding Nature's Intent

Nature, in its essence, is a force that drives evolution and change. It is not just about the physical environment around us but encompasses the broader aspects of existence, including our experiences, emotions, and the spiritual journey we undertake. The role of nature, as I perceive it, is to facilitate our evolution, both as individuals and as a collective consciousness.

One of the fundamental aspects of nature's design is its propensity to keep us engaged in the orbit of duality. Our lives are replete with contrasts - joy and sorrow, success and failure, love and loss. This duality is not a mere coincidence; it is a deliberate aspect of the simulation we are part of. It keeps us anchored in the material world, ensuring that our journey is dynamic and filled with learning experiences.

However, I firmly believe that living a material life is not inherently negative. Our physical reality is our domain of experience, where we learn, grow, and evolve. To dismiss the material world as an illusion or a distraction from spiritual growth is to miss the essence of our existence. We are here to experience life in all its dimensions, to embrace the joys and challenges that come our way.

Some of us might contemplate abandoning our worldly lives in pursuit of spirituality, perhaps in the solitude of the mountains. While this search for spiritual enlightenment is a noble path, it's crucial to recognize that the nature of desire remains unchanged. Whether it's the longing for material possessions or the yearning for spiritual liberation, the underlying emotion is desire. In my perspective, transcending this desire is not about physically removing oneself from the world but about changing one's approach to life.

I advocate a simple yet profound approach to life: live it as it comes, fulfilling your duties and responsibilities, adhering to the universal laws that govern our existence. Acceptance is key. Accept the experiences that life brings, the good and the bad, and find contentment in them. This acceptance is not passive; it's an active engagement with life, an acknowledgment of its ebbs and flows.

True meditation, as I understand it, is not just a practice of sitting in silence; it is the art of living life in its entirety. It is about being present in every moment, embracing each experience with an open heart and a calm mind. It's about finding peace in the chaos of life, harmony in its contradictions.

Imagine being like water, flowing effortlessly in the direction the river takes. When we attempt to swim against the current, we might find ourselves struggling and eventually wearing out. This struggle is akin to resisting the natural flow of life, the path that nature or the creator has intended for us.

Consider the life of a fish, for which the entire existence is water. A fish doesn't concern itself with what lies beyond its aquatic world; its life is entirely within the bounds of its watery world. Similarly, we are elements within this vast cosmos, a cosmos that has been meticulously crafted by the creator. For us, life in this universe is what water is to the fish.

This analogy leads us to a profound understanding: just as a fish thrives in water, we too are meant to thrive within the parameters set by this universe. Our existence, our reality, is defined by the cosmic laws and the environment we inhabit. When we align ourselves with these cosmic rhythms, we find our natural course, much like a river finding its way to the sea.

To flow like water means to embrace the

journey of life with all its twists and turns, highs and lows. It means accepting the course of our lives as it unfolds, trusting in the universal plan set out for us. This doesn't imply passivity or resignation; rather, it's an active acceptance, a conscious choice to flow with life's currents.

This approach to life encourages us to be adaptable, resilient, and open to change. Like water that molds itself according to the landscape, we too can learn to adapt to the varying circumstances of our lives. This adaptability is a form of strength, an ability to maintain our essence while being flexible enough to navigate life's changes.

The Cosmic Brain: Parallels Between the Human Mind and the Universe

Recently, I came across a fascinating piece of information that struck a chord with me: the structure of our universe bears a remarkable resemblance to the human brain. This discovery piqued my curiosity, and I felt compelled to share it. The idea that the architecture of our brain might mirror that of the universe is not merely poetic; it's a hypothesis grounded in scientific observations. This concept made me wonder: could it be that the creator designed our brain in the image of the universe, or are we, perhaps, a fragment of the creator's cosmic mind, where universes like ours are born from their imagination?

Recent scientific endeavors, particularly those involving the cerebral cortex and cerebellum, have drawn comparisons to images captured by advanced telescopes like the James Webb. The parallels they've found are not superficial but deeply rooted in the structural and functional similarities between these two seemingly disparate entities.

Consider this: each neuron in our brain could be likened to a galaxy within the vast expanse of the universe. The way galaxies are interlinked by cosmic filaments mirrors how neurons are connected through a complex network of dendrites and axons. These connections are crucial, facilitating the flow of information and energy that is vital for both the operations of the universe and the workings of the human mind.

During these studies, researchers observed that the arrangement and interconnections of neurons closely resemble the distribution and networking of galaxies. This similarity extends beyond mere appearance to the intricate ways these structures interact and form complex networks.

This realization brings us to a profound understanding of our existence. The brain, our center for thought, emotion, and perception, seems to reflect the structure of the cosmos itself. This parallel suggests that the universe, in all its complexity and enigma, is mirrored within us. We are not merely occupants of the universe; we are, in a sense, a miniature representation of it.

Chapter 10

Time and Space: Illusions in the Cosmic Play, but Absolute in Our Reality

The perception of time and space has long been a subject of intrigue and debate in both scientific and philosophical circles. In the grand scheme of the universe, time, especially from the perspective of its creator, may be nothing more than an illusion, a malleable construct rather than a fixed continuum. For the avatars within this universe – entities like us – time and space assume a critical, tangible role, integral to the very fabric of our existence.

For the creator of the universe, time could be perceived as a nonlinear dimension, an aspect that can be manipulated, traversed, or even transcended. This view aligns with several traditional and modern theories which postulate that time and space, as we understand them, are not absolute constructs but relative perceptions. In this broader, cosmic perspective, the past, present, and future might coexist, observable simultaneously much like a vast tapestry viewed from a distance.

However, for the inhabitants of this universe – the avatars – time and space take on a distinct and practical significance. In our simulated world, these dimensions form the backbone of our reality. They dictate the rhythm of our lives, the progression of our experiences, and the framework within which we operate. From this vantage point, time flows in a linear fashion, and space provides the stage upon which the events of the universe unfold.

The creator, in designing this universe, has ingeniously programmed time and space to have specific roles and values. For the avatars, these dimensions are not mere illusions but the parameters that define their existence. They influence everything from the physical laws that govern movement and growth to the personal experiences of aging, learning, and memory.

We also examine how this concept of time and space as illusions, yet realities, has been echoed in various scientific and philosophical doctrines. From the relativistic theories of Einstein, which revolutionized our understanding of these dimensions, to ancient philosophical teachings that view time as a cyclical or illusory concept, we see a recurring theme – the fluidity and complexity of time and space.

Furthermore, this exploration invites us to reflect on the implications of living in a universe where time and space, while seemingly absolute to us, are potentially malleable from a higher perspective. What does this mean for our concepts of destiny, free will, and the nature of reality? How does it shape our understanding of life, growth, and the progression of the cosmos?

Perceptions of Time and Dimensions

This section explores into the intriguing notion that not only is our experience of time and dimensions different from that of the cosmic creator, but also that each individual. I cannot offer concrete evidence to substantiate this; it might merely be a product of my imagination, yet I propose that the timelines for every individual – be it myself, you, or your family members – differ distinctively. While we might all perceive the illusion of sharing the same 24-hour day, the reality of time and space is altered by various factors including our thoughts, our physical mass, the gravitational pull, and the positioning of celestial bodies.

Consider the experience of time in moments of joy and sorrow. When we are happy and immersed in enjoyable activities, time seems to accelerate, with hours feeling like minutes. Conversely, in periods of sadness or grief, time appears to decelerate, with each minute stretching out painfully. This contrast in time perception under different emotional states points to the subjective nature of time – a fluid, malleable experience rather than a rigid, unchanging constant.

Moreover, the theory of relativity in physics supports the idea that time and space are interwoven and influenced by mass and gravity. This scientific principle suggests that the gravitational pull of planetary bodies can alter the flow of time – a concept that resonates with certain astrological beliefs. Astrology posits that celestial bodies exert invisible forces on our lives, influencing our destinies and personal experiences, including our perception of time.

This idea extends beyond the monarchy of human experience to encompass all entities in the universe. Each living and non-living thing, governed by its unique set of circumstances and cosmic influences, experiences time differently. For instance, the lifespan of a tree spans centuries, with its perception of time vastly different from that of a human. Similarly, animals, insects, and even inanimate objects like mountains and rivers exist in their distinct temporal domains.

The concept of individual timelines within the broader cosmic timeline is a fascinating aspect of this discussion. Each soul, each entity, navigates through its unique timeline, experiencing the universe in a way that is intimately personal and distinct. This individuality of time experience underscores the diversity and complexity of the universe – a tapestry woven from countless threads of unique temporal experiences.

The Yuga Cycle: A Reflection on Time and Transformation

In the rich tapestry of Hindu mythology, the concept of the Yuga cycle presents a fascinating view of time and cosmic evolution. This cycle is divided into four distinct phases: Satyuga, Treta Yuga, Dwapar Yuga, and Kaliyuga. Each Yuga is characterized by its own set of principles and challenges, shaping the course of human history and consciousness. However, surrounding these Yugas are various myths and interpretations, some linked to karma, others to the balance of truth and falsehood. Yet, at their core, these cycles revolve around the evolution of human intellect and consciousness.

As I navigated through various sources to deepen my understanding of the Yuga cycle, I encountered a plethora of interpretations and viewpoints, many of which seemed to diverge from the essence of the concept. One common misconception, often found in online sources including Wikipedia, is the notion that we are currently living in Kaliyuga, the age of darkness and decline. However, my study and understanding of these cycles suggest a different narrative.

Satyuga, the first in the cycle, is often referred to as the Golden Age, a time when truth, righteousness, and virtue reign supreme. It is an era where human beings live in harmony with nature and each other, guided by high spiritual and moral standards. As the cycle progresses into

Treta Yuga and Dwapar Yuga, there is a gradual decline in these virtues, with each age witnessing a diminishing adherence to truth and righteousness.

Kaliyuga, often portrayed as the darkest phase, is characterized by strife, discord, and a general decline in moral and spiritual values. It is believed that during this time, human beings are farthest from divine principles, engulfed in materialism and ignorance. However, this traditional view of Kaliyuga is not the only perspective.

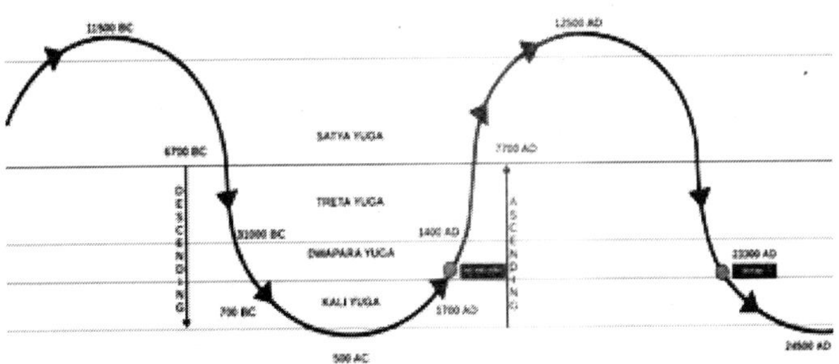

My exploration led me to a different understanding of the current age. Contrary to the popular belief in our descent into Kaliyuga, I perceive that we are, in fact, transitioning out of it, moving towards a new Satyuga. This transition is marked not by observable external changes but by a subtle yet profound shift in human consciousness and intellect. It is a shift towards greater awareness, compassion, and a deeper understanding of our connection with the cosmos.

This perspective on the Yuga cycle is more than just a chronological account of ages; it is a reflection on the evolution of human consciousness. Each Yuga represents not only a period in time but also a state of collective human consciousness.

I have included a diagram to provide a clearer understanding of this intricate cycle. Through my research, I have come to the conclusion that we have recently transitioned into Dwapar Yuga. According to the timeline presented in the diagram, we exited Kaliyuga around the year 1700 AD. The period before this, stretching back to

700 BC, was marked by strife and darkness, characteristics typically associated with Kaliyuga. Historical accounts from this era often recount tales of wars and societal turmoil.

If we think logically about the progression of human history, significant advancements such as the invention of electric lighting, the development of automobiles, and the formulation of the theory of evolution all started to emerge after 1700 AD. This period marks a significant shift in human consciousness and technological development, aligning with the transition into Dwapar Yuga.

In my initial chapters, I discussed how the current age of AI and the Metaverse represents a new beginning in human advancement. I foresee this era of technological and intellectual growth continuing for the next 10,000 years, during which humanity will progress through various stages of artificial intelligence development.

However, after the year 12500 AD, a gradual decline in human intellect and spiritual awareness is predicted, eventually leading to a point where the universe undergoes a reset. This reset should not be misconstrued as an apocalypse or doom; rather, it is a natural part of the cyclical nature of our universe. It's a process through which civilizations reach their peak of advancement and then start anew. This cyclical pattern is evident in the rise and fall of ancient civilizations like the Egyptian and Indus Valley civilizations, which advanced significantly before eventually fading into history.

As I explore the historical events and technological advancements that align with the transition from Kaliyuga to Dwapar Yuga, emphasizing the correlation between these cosmic cycles and human progress.

Chapter 11

Karma: Unveiling Its Essence in the Cosmic Scheme

The notion of karma, a ubiquitous term in discussions surrounding God, spirituality, and the laws of the universe, evokes a range of reactions and beliefs. Often enveloped in a shroud of mystery and misunderstanding, karma is a concept that seems to resonate universally, yet is interpreted in myriad ways. This exploration looks into the depths of karma, seeking to understand its true significance, its operation in our lives, and the reasons behind its profound impact on human consciousness.

Karma, traditionally understood in many cultures, particularly in Eastern philosophies, is often viewed as a cosmic law of cause and effect. It's a principle that suggests every action has a corresponding reaction, and that the deeds of an individual will inevitably shape their future. However, the interpretation and perception of karma extend beyond this simplistic cause-and-effect framework, touching upon the very essence of human existence and the nature of the universe.

In everyday life, people frequently reference karma in the context of morality and justice. When someone commits a wrongdoing, it's common to hear phrases like "karma will catch up with them." Conversely, when experiencing hardship or misfortune, individuals often question whether it's a result of their past actions – their karma. This dichotomy in perception – viewing karma as both a punishing force and a moral compass – raises intriguing questions about its role in our lives.

The discussion of karma often leads to the philosophical debate on illusion versus reality. In moments of self-reflection or guilt, individuals might dismiss the world and its happenings as mere illusions. Yet, when faced with injustice or suffering, the same individuals might find the concept of karma very tangible and significant. This selective perception of karma, oscillating between illusion and reality, reveals deeper layers of human psychology and spirituality.

To understand the workings of karma, it's imperative to look at it not just as a religious or philosophical concept but as a fundamental aspect of the cosmic order. Karma can be seen as a mechanism that maintains balance and harmony in the universe. It's not merely a punitive system but a self-regulating process that ensures the continuity and progression of life and consciousness.

At its core, karma is about responsibility and interconnectedness. It teaches that every individual, through their thoughts, words, and actions, contributes to the fabric of the universe. This interconnected web of actions and reactions creates a dynamic, ever-evolving tapestry of existence. Karma, in this sense, is a reminder of our role in this vast cosmic play, urging us to be mindful of our contributions to the world.

Moreover, the concept of karma challenges the notion of an external, judgmental deity dictating our fate. Instead, it places the power and responsibility in our own hands, suggesting that we are the architects of our destiny. This perspective empowers individuals to take control of their lives, understanding that their current circumstances are a reflection of their past actions and that their future is in their making.

The exploration of karma also intersects with scientific principles, particularly in the field of quantum mechanics, where the observer's consciousness influences the observed phenomenon. This correlation between observation and outcome in the quantum world mirrors the principle of karma, where intention and action influence future outcomes.

The traditional interpretation of karma is rooted in the idea that every action inevitably leads to a reaction. This view, while holding a kernel of truth, is a simplified rendition of a more complex, nuanced principle. To gain a fuller understanding, let's consider a simulated universe, akin to the one I designed. In this virtual world, avatars are endowed with consciousness and awareness, enabling them to make choices and perform actions. Now, imagine embedding an additional code into this simulation – a code dictating that for every action an avatar takes, there will be a corresponding response, governed by the simulation itself.

This scenario is not just a flight of fancy but a plausible model for understanding the deeper dynamics of karma. In this simulated universe, every choice and action of an avatar sets off a chain of events, each with its consequences. The simulation, running on the principles embedded by its creator, ensures that these consequences are in line with the actions taken. This mechanism mirrors the essential concept of karma – a self-regulating, responsive system where actions determine outcomes.

But karma, in its true essence, extends beyond this. It's not just about actions and their immediate responses; it's about the accumulation of these actions over time and their cumulative impact on the avatar's journey within the simulation. This perspective of karma involves a broader understanding of time and continuity, where the effects of actions may manifest not immediately but over a course of events, shaping the avatar's experiences and circumstances.

Furthermore, karma in this simulated world isn't merely a punitive or rewarding mechanism. It's a guiding force that encourages learning, growth, and evolution. As avatars navigate this world, their actions lead to experiences that foster understanding, wisdom, and development. This growth-oriented aspect of karma is crucial – it suggests that the primary purpose of karma is not to judge or recompense but to facilitate progression and enlightenment.

The concept of karma also ties in with the notion of free will and destiny. In our simulated universe, while the avatars are conscious and capable of making choices, their environment and the fundamental laws governing the simulation limit these choices. This interplay between free will and predetermined rules reflects the delicate balance between autonomy and destiny in the orbit of karma. It suggests that while we are free to choose our actions, the consequences are bound by the cosmic laws set in motion by the universe's creator.

To further understand karma, we also need to consider the collective aspect. In our simulated world, the actions of one avatar can affect others, creating a web of interconnectivity. This interconnectedness is a vital component of karma, where individual actions contribute to a larger, communal narrative. It emphasizes the significance of our actions not just for ourselves but for the collective whole.

Karma, in this context, also resonates

with the principles of modern science, particularly in the fields of quantum physics and systems theory. These scientific disciplines explore how individual components of a system (or particles in the quantum region) interact and influence the system as a whole. This scientific parallel offers a contemporary lens through which we can view the ancient concept of karma.

Conundrums of Perception: Decoding Reality in the Quantum Age

The world as we perceive it, entrenched in stability and continuity, is fundamentally a derivation of classical physics. This paradigm paints the universe as a colossal, well-oiled machine, operating with unwavering predictability. In this deterministic view, every occurrence is the result of a preceding cause, establishing a clear chain of cause and effect. Yet, as we look deeper into the field of atomic theory and quantum mechanics, this linear perspective begins to disintegrate, revealing a universe teeming with endless possibilities and probabilities.

In the microscopic domain governed by quantum mechanics, conventional norms of classical physics find no foothold. Particles like electrons and photons exist in a haze of probabilities, refusing to commit to a definitive state until they are observed or interacted with. This quantum conundrum radically challenges our traditional understanding of reality. The universe, which appears solid and consistent to our physical senses, is essentially a vast ocean of potentialities at its most elemental level. The present, seemingly definitive and concrete, is merely one among myriad potential outcomes birthed from the past.

The peculiar nature of quantum reality, exemplified in experiments like the double-slit experiment, illustrates this beautifully.

Photons display dual characteristics – as particles and waves. Unobserved, they create wave-like interference patterns. However, upon observation, they adopt particle-like behaviors, impacting specific points like discrete entities. This dual behavior of photons is a metaphor for the dual nature of reality itself – malleable, changeable, and influenced by observation.

This quantum perspective extends beyond the behaviors of subatomic particles in controlled laboratory environments. It permeates to the core of our understanding of the universe. The principle of superposition, a cornerstone of quantum mechanics, posits that particles can simultaneously exist in multiple states until they are observed. This principle draws a parallel to the philosophical thought experiment of Schrödinger's cat, which exists in a state of life and death simultaneously until observed.

Such quantum implications profoundly impact our perception of reality. They suggest a universe not rigidly chained to cause and effect but woven from a tapestry of probabilities. This shift in understanding not only revolutionizes our grasp of physics but also bears significant philosophical implications regarding free will, determinism, and the essence of existence.

In our daily existence, the quantum view of reality reflects in the decisions we make. Each choice is a superposition of possibilities, with the path we choose collapsing these possibilities into a singular reality. The paths not taken linger as unmanifested potentials, akin to the unobserved states in quantum mechanics.

Moreover, we investigate into how these scientific principles resonate with philosophical and existential questions that have long fascinated humanity. The quantum view of reality offers a fresh perspective for pondering the universe's mysteries and our role within it. It suggests that understanding the world involves not just observation and measurement but also participation and influence in the fabric of reality.

For humans, often swayed by the teachings of scientists, philosophers, and spiritual gurus, this quantum perspective presents a profound shift. From the vantage point of the universe's creator, time and reality may be fluid, a simultaneous coexistence of past, present, and future. For us, the avatars within this cosmic simulation, time and space are experienced linearly, with each moment unfolding from the last. This dichotomy between the creator's perception and our lived experience forms the crux of our exploration in this chapter.

As we traverse through these complex themes, we gain not just scientific insight but also a deeper philosophical understanding of our universe. This exploration is not merely an academic endeavor; it's a journey into the heart of existence, inviting us to reconsider our assumptions about the world and embrace the quantum field's endless possibilities. By the end of this chapter, readers will emerge with a more nuanced understanding of reality, transcending traditional confines and venturing into a domain where the only certainty is the boundless potential of the quantum universe.

How Karma Actually Works: Cause,Effect and Consequence

"Karma" – a concept deeply ingrained in various philosophies and spiritual teachings – often gets simplified as a straightforward equation of cause and effect. However, this interpretation barely scratches the surface of its profound complexity. To truly understand karma, one must explore the additional layer of consequences that stem from every cause and the ensuing actions. In this extensive exploration, we look into the intricate workings of karma, weaving philosophical examples to illuminate its nuanced dynamics.

At its core, the principle of karma involves a sequence of actions, reactions, and repercussions. For every action (the cause), there is an immediate effect, but more importantly, there is a consequence – a ripple that extends far beyond the initial impact. These consequences can be subtle or significant, immediate or delayed, but they are always inevitably linked to the originating action.

Consider a morally charged action, such as causing harm to another person. The immediate effect is clear – harm is inflicted, pain is caused. But the consequences of this action extend beyond the act itself. The emotional turmoil, the psychological scars left on the victim's loved ones, and the societal ripples all contribute to a complex web of results that go far beyond the simple act of harm.

These consequences are not always predictable or linear. The law of karma suggests that our actions set into motion a series of events that eventually circle back to us. This circularity is crucial in understanding karma. It's not merely about retribution or a cosmic balancing act; it's about understanding the interconnectedness of our actions and their far-reaching impacts.

Furthermore, the idea that karma's consequences might lie dormant before manifesting challenges the notion of immediate justice or visible retribution. It introduces a temporal dimension to karma, where the seeds of an action may take time to germinate and bear fruit. This aspect of karma is where many misconceptions arise. People often mistakenly believe that if the consequences of an action are not immediate or apparent, they are non-existent. However, the teachings of karma emphasize that every action has its corresponding reaction, even if it is not immediately evident.

To better understand this, let's explore a simple yet profound example: the act of telling a lie. The immediate effect of lying might be the avoidance of a problem or the gaining of an advantage. However, the consequences of this dishonesty are manifold. Trust is eroded, relationships are strained, and the integrity of the liar is compromised. Over time, these consequences manifest in various ways, affecting not just the liar but also those around them.

The concept of karma also ties into the philosophical idea of moral responsibility. Our actions, driven by our intentions and decisions, are a reflection of our moral and ethical stance. Karma teaches that we are not just passive recipients of fate; we are active participants in shaping our destiny and the world around us.

In addition to personal actions, karma also encompasses collective actions. The decisions made by communities, societies, and nations create collective karma, influencing the course of history and the lives of countless individuals. The consequences of collective actions often manifest as social, political, and environmental changes, impacting generations.

Moreover, we examine how the understanding of karma can be applied in our daily lives. By becoming more aware of the consequences of our actions, we can make more conscious choices, leading to a life that is in harmony with the principles of karma. This awareness also fosters a deeper sense of empathy and understanding, as we recognize the interconnectedness of all beings and the shared impact of our actions.

The Mechanics of Luck: A Personal Exploration

In my journey of understanding the intricate tapestry of life, I've often pondered over the concept of luck. Is luck merely a random occurrence, a fortunate roll of the cosmic dice, or is there a deeper mechanism at play? As I previously discussed the triad of cause, effect, and consequence in the context of karma, I find myself drawn to the idea that luck, too, operates within this framework. In this section, I will explore the notion that what we often attribute to luck is, in fact, the outcome of a sequence of causes and their ensuing consequences, some of which stem from actions in the distant past.

The common perception of luck is as a mysterious force that randomly blesses or curses individuals. We hear people say, "He's so lucky, he always lands on his feet," or "She must be lucky to have achieved so much." However, upon closer examination, I propose that luck is not an arbitrary force but a complex interplay of actions and reactions, with roots often buried deep in past events.

To understand this concept, let's consider the idea that every action sets off a chain of events – a series of causes and effects. These chains, over time, weave together to create the tapestry of our lives. The 'luck' that we experience is often the visible outcome of these intricate, interconnected chains. What appears to be a sudden stroke of fortune or misfortune is, in reality, the culmination of various factors converging at a point in time.

Take, for instance, the story of a successful entrepreneur. To an outside observer, their success might seem like a stroke of luck. But delving deeper into their journey reveals a series of strategic decisions, hard work, and perhaps a few fortuitous opportunities that they capitalized on. Their 'luck' was not a random gift from the universe but the result of their actions and choices.

Similarly, in our own lives, we might attribute certain outcomes to luck without recognizing the underlying causes. The chance meeting that leads to a significant opportunity, the unexpected windfall, the narrow escape from danger – these instances of 'luck' are interwoven with our past actions and decisions.

The concept of luck also ties into the idea of synchronicity. Carl Jung, the Swiss psychiatrist, introduced this concept to describe events that are meaningfully related yet lack an apparent causal connection. Synchronicity suggests that there is a deeper order to the universe, where seemingly random events are connected in a way that transcends conventional notions of cause and effect.

Different cultures have various beliefs and superstitions surrounding luck, from lucky charms and rituals to the idea of fate and destiny. These cultural interpretations provide insight into humanity's enduring fascination with and attempts to understand the elusive nature of luck.

Furthermore, I reflect on the practical implications of this understanding of luck. Recognizing the role of past actions in shaping current outcomes empowers us to take responsibility for our lives. It encourages us to make conscious choices, knowing that these decisions contribute to the 'luck' we will encounter in the future.

There is a fine line between relying on luck and taking proactive steps in life. While acknowledging the role of luck, it is crucial not to fall into passivity, waiting for fortune to smile upon us. Active engagement with life, combined with an awareness of the underlying currents that shape our destiny, is the key to navigating the uncertain waters of existence.

CHAPTER 12

CONCLUDING REFLECTIONS

As I approach the conclusion of this book, I find myself reflecting on the nature of the spiritual journey, a path as unique and individual as each one of us. My experiences and explorations have led me to a simple yet profound realization: true spiritual growth is a deeply personal experience, one that cannot be fully understood or replicated through the experiences of others. While we can draw inspiration and guidance from the journeys of others, our path must be our own.

Throughout my life, I have been on a relentless search for understanding and enlightenment. This journey has taken me through various spheres of thought and philosophy, from the intricate teachings of ancient scriptures to the profound simplicity of nature's laws. What I have come to understand is that the core of spiritual wisdom is not hidden in complex texts or esoteric doctrines; it is found in the simple and the everyday.

The universal laws that govern our existence, the principles that underpin the cosmos, are surprisingly straightforward and accessible. They are evident in the natural world around us, in the rhythm of the seasons, the balance of ecosystems, and the basic principles of kindness and compassion that resonate within each of us. To comprehend these laws, one does not need to explore into dense philosophical treatises. Instead, it requires an open heart and a keen observation of the world.

In this journey, I have learned the importance of acceptance. Accepting things as they are, without resistance or denial, is a fundamental principle of spiritual harmony. This acceptance is not a passive resignation but an active acknowledgment of the flow of life. It is about aligning ourselves with the natural order of things, understanding that we are part of a larger whole.

Another key lesson has been the value of calmness and simplicity. In a world that often values complexity and constant activity, finding peace in simplicity can be a transformative experience. Keeping the mind calm and uncluttered allows us to see things more clearly, to understand the subtle messages of the universe, and to connect more deeply with our inner selves.

As I continue my journey, I am aware

that I am still seeking, still learning. There are many answers I have yet to find, many truths yet to be uncovered. However, this ongoing search is not a source of frustration but a wellspring of joy and wonder. It is a journey that is as rewarding as it is challenging.

As I share these reflections with you, my hope is that they serve not as definitive answers but as signposts on your own journey. Each person's spiritual path is unique, shaped by their experiences, beliefs, and insights. What works for one may not work for another. But in sharing our journeys, we can offer each other support, inspiration, and a sense of shared purpose.

At the beginning of this book, I introduced concepts like AI and the Metaverse, primarily to lay a foundation for understanding how the creator of the universe might have designed us. It's equally important, however, to explore what the future might hold in store with these technologies. As I sit down to share my thoughts on the future, particularly in the context of rapidly evolving technologies like AI and the Metaverse, I am struck by a sense of anticipation mixed with responsibility. Often, I find people around me expressing apprehension towards these new technologies. However, from my perspective, the current iterations of AI and other technological advancements represent just the nascent stages of a much more profound evolution. We are at the beginning of a journey that promises to reshape our world in ways we are only beginning to comprehend.

In my view, the future, as influenced by technological progression, holds immense potential for positive change. One of the areas where I foresee significant impact is in addressing environmental challenges. With advanced AI and other emerging technologies, we have the tools to develop more sustainable ways of living, potentially reversing some of the damage inflicted on our planet. This prospect fills me with hope, as it aligns with the universal law that dictates evolution and growth over time.

Moreover, the advancement in technology, especially in the field of healthcare, offers promising solutions to myriad diseases that plague humanity today. I envision a future where illnesses that are currently incurable become easily treatable, thanks to breakthroughs in medical technology driven by AI and other innovations.

This progress, I believe, is not happening in isolation or by mere chance. It aligns with the will of the creator, the universal force that sowed the seeds of these technologies. In my chapter on Yugas, I discussed the cyclical ages in Hindu cosmology. Currently, as per my understanding, we are transitioning into Satyug – an era of truth and enlightenment where human intellect and consciousness are set to expand exponentially. This transition marks the beginning of a 10,000-year cycle where we, as a species, are likely to experience significant intellectual and spiritual growth.

With the rise in human intellect and the advancement of technology, I foresee a transformation in our lifestyle and societal structures. This is not just about technological gadgets or sophisticated AI systems; it's about a fundamental shift in how we perceive our existence and our role in the universe. The future holds a new way of living, where technology and spirituality coalesce, leading to a more enlightened, connected, and compassionate society.

Furthermore, as technology progresses, I predict that we will see a blurring of lines between physical and digital realities. The Metaverse, a concept that is currently in its infancy, will likely become an integral part of our daily lives. It will offer new dimensions of interaction, learning, and experiencing the world, transcending physical boundaries and opening up new worlds of possibilities.

This evolution, however, comes with its set of challenges and ethical considerations. As we advance technologically, we must remain vigilant about the implications of these technologies on our privacy, freedom, and the very essence of what it means to be human. The future will require us to navigate these challenges with wisdom, foresight, and a deep sense of responsibility.

It's a reflection of my belief that we are on the cusp of a transformative era, one that will redefine our existence and propel us towards a more enlightened, technologically advanced, and interconnected world. This vision of the future is not just a prediction; it's a call to action for us to shape this emerging world responsibly, guided by the principles of sustainability, compassion, and universal harmony.

THE COSMIC CYCLE: CONTEMPLATING THE END OF THE UNIVERSE

In the early pages of this book, I touched upon the rise and fall of advanced civilizations, a recurring theme in the tapestry of time. These civilizations, once at the pinnacle of their existence, eventually succumbed to the inevitable flow of time, leaving behind echoes of their presence. This cyclical nature of creation and dissolution, I believe, is a fundamental aspect of the universe's design. The universe, as it stands, is programmed for a reset, a concept deeply rooted in the ancient philosophy of Yugas, which I discussed earlier.

We currently find ourselves in the nascent stages of Satyuga, a period marked by truth, righteousness, and spiritual awakening. This era, extending over the next 10,000 years, is one of evolution and enlightenment. It is a time where humanity will reach new heights of intellect and understanding. However, this upward trajectory is not without its culmination point.

My contemplation leads me to a profound hypothesis: the universe, in its infinite wisdom, has set in motion a self-regulating mechanism. At the zenith of our intellectual and spiritual journey, when we begin to simply the mechanics of the creator or start tampering with the fundamental laws of physics, a reset becomes imminent. This is not a punishment or a whimsical act of a capricious deity but a necessary process in the cosmic cycle.

The end of the universe, or rather its reset, is not an event to be feared but a part of the natural order. It's a reminder of the impermanence of everything, urging us to cherish the present and strive for meaningful contributions that transcend our physical existence. It encourages us to focus on spiritual growth and understanding, aligning ourselves with the universal laws that govern our existence.

This is not a prediction of doom but a meditation on the universe's innate wisdom and its cyclical nature.

Note